Jehovah's Witness Literature

A Critical Guide to Watchtower Publications

David A. Reed

BAKER
A DIVISION OF
Baker Book House Co

© 1993 by David A. Reed

Published by Baker Books
a division of Baker Book House Company
P.O. Box 6287, Grand Rapids, MI 49516-6287

ISBN: 0-8010-7768-0

Second printing, December 1994

Printed in the United States of America

Unless otherwise noted, all Scripture references are taken from the New World Translation (NWT), King James Version (KJV), or the New American Standard Bible (NASB), © the Lockman Foundation 1960, 1962, 1963, 1968, 1971, 1972, 1973, 1975, 1977.

Jehovah's
Witness
Literature

"Of making many books there is no end."

Ecclesiastes 12:12

Contents

Introduction

At some point during the late 1980s Jehovah's Witnesses published their 10-billionth (10,000,000,000th) piece of literature. It took more than one hundred years to produce all those books, booklets, magazines, and tracts since the first *Watch Tower* magazine rolled off the press in the summer of 1879, but the next 10 billion pieces of literature may take little more than a decade, if the sect continues to grow at its present rate.

With a twice-monthly printing in excess of 16 million copies per issue, *The Watchtower* magazine now approaches the circulation of such all-time favorites as *Reader's Digest* and *T.V. Guide* and easily outsells the combined total of *Time, Newsweek,* and *U.S. News & World Report.*

The *1991 Yearbook of Jehovah's Witnesses* reports more than eleven thousand full-time factory and office workers (up from five thousand in 1980). The January 1, 1993 *Watchtower* reports nearly 4.5 million active participants in the work of distributing literature from house to house worldwide. Some 11.5 million people are to be found at kingdom halls studying Watchtower literature.

Compared with a half-billion Muslims or Hindus or Roman Catholics, the Jehovah's Witness sect is still very small, but its influence is way out of proportion to its numbers. Indeed, in many lands nearly the entire population receives visits from the Witnesses, and they produce enough literature to supply most of the world. In fact, that is precisely their aim: to reach everyone on earth with "this good news of the kingdom" (Matt. 24:14 *New World Translation*).

But in quoting Matthew 24:14 or reading it aloud, Jehovah's Witnesses will often put their vocal emphasis on the word *this* rather than on *good news* or *kingdom*. They are making the point that the good news or gospel they are preaching is "*this* good news," different from what others have preached over the centuries since Christ:

> The Kingdom witnessing of Jehovah's Witnesses since 1914 has been something far different from what Christendom's missionaries have published both before and since 1914. "Different"—how so? . . . the preaching of this good news of the Messianic kingdom as having been established in the heavens in 1914. (*The Watchtower*, October 1, 1980, pp. 28–29)

Briefly, "this" good news or gospel is the teaching that Jesus Christ (who is not deity, in JW theology, but the first created angel) returned invisibly in 1914 and put the Watchtower organization in charge of his interests, pending the battle of Armageddon, during which he will soon destroy everyone else on earth and leave only Jehovah's Witnesses alive to transform the planet into paradise.

The problem with "this" gospel is that it is not the original one preached by the twelve apostles. So these words of Paul apply:

> But though we, or an angel from heaven, preach any other gospel unto you than that which we have preached unto you, let him be accursed. (Gal. 1:8 KJV)

Since the abundance of literature produced and circulated around the world by Jehovah's Witnesses is devoted to spreading another gospel, one different from the biblical gospel of Christ, those lured into distributing this material are in a dangerous position.

In view of the fact that JW literature is the chief means of propagating this false gospel, Christians engaged in defending the faith cannot afford to be ignorant of the books and magazines being delivered to their doors and to the doors of their relatives, friends, and neighbors. As Paul quoted Greek altar inscriptions and "your own poets" when he talked to the men of Athens, we may find it helpful to be familiar with what the Watchtower has written when we talk with Jehovah's Witnesses (Acts 17:23, 28). But, since the sheer volume of such material is overwhelming, a guide to Jehovah's Witness literature is needed. This book is intended to meet that need.

1

Origins

"The special messenger to the last Age of the Church was Charles T. Russell, born February 16, 1852. He has privately admitted his belief that he was chosen for his great work from before his birth." Thus begins a brief biographical sketch of the founder of the Jehovah's Witness sect in Studies in the Scriptures, vol. 7, *The Finished Mystery* (1917 edition, p. 53). The 1918 Karatol edition of this same work lists "The Seven Messengers to the Church" as "St. Paul, St. John, Arius, Waldo, Wycliffe, Luther, Russell" (p. 64). These remarks explain the importance attached to Russell's writings by those who rank him with the apostles Paul and John.

How did he make the move from membership in a mainline denomination to leadership of a new sect that today draws 11.5 million followers to its meetings? *The Finished Mystery* goes on to quote from autobiographical remarks Russell published in *The Watchtower:*

> We begin the narrative at the year 1868, when the Editor, having been a consecrated child of God for some years, and a member of the Congregational Church and of the Y.M.C.A., began to be shaken in faith regarding many long accepted doctrines. Brought up a Presbyterian, indoctrinated from the catechism, and being naturally of an inquiring mind, I fell a ready prey to

the logic of infidelity, as soon as I began to think for myself. But that which at first threatened to be the utter shipwreck of faith in God and the Bible, was, under God's providence, over-ruled for good, and merely wrecked my confidence in human creeds and systems of Bible interpretations. . . . for the first time, I heard something of the views of Second Adventism, by Jonas Wendell, long since deceased. Thus I confess indebtedness to Adventists as well as to other Bible students.[1]

Early in 1876 Russell came into possession of a copy of the Second Adventist magazine *The Herald of the Morning,* published by N. H. Barbour of Rochester, New York. Spiritual descendants of the Millerites, who had expected Christ's return in 1844, the Second Adventists had expected the second coming to occur in 1874, but were likewise disappointed. Barbour, however, refused to accept such a disappointment; he chose instead to proclaim that Christ did indeed return in 1874, only invisible to human eyes. He based his argument on Benjamin Wilson's *Emphatic Diaglott,* a Greek interlinear New Testament in which the translator, a member of the Church of God (Faith of Abraham), rendered Christ's *coming* at Matthew 24:27, 37, and 39 as *presence,* which Barbour interpreted as an invisible presence.

Meeting with Barbour in Philadelphia, Russell offered him badly needed financial backing, in exchange for which he was added to the staff of the Second Adventist magazine *The Herald of the Morning* as an assistant editor. And the following year, at the age of twenty-five, Russell helped Barbour complete and publish a book called *Three Worlds, or Plan of Redemption.*

A couple of years later, however, Russell came into conflict with Barbour over the doctrine of Christ's ransom. Intent on publishing his own views, Russell resigned his post as an assistant editor of *The Herald of the Morning* and in July 1879 released the first issue of his own religious magazine, *Zion's Watch Tower and Herald of Christ's Presence.* He took with him a number of Second Adventist followers who believed that "Pastor Russell took the place of Mr. Barbour who became unfaithful and upon whom was fulfilled the prophecies of Matthew 24:48–51 and Zechariah 11:15–17."[2]

Zion's Watch Tower served as the rallying point for followers Russell accumulated through his dynamic public speaking in city after city. And when he began to write a series of books outlining his theology, the magazine proved to be an effective advertising medium. Not merely a writer and preacher, however, Russell was also an apt organizer and administrator. During 1879 and 1880 he organized "some thirty congregations in Pennsylvania, New Jersey, New York, Massachusetts, Delaware, Ohio and Michigan," personally visiting each group of *Watch Tower* subscribers (*1975 Yearbook of Jehovah's Witnesses,* p. 39). His aim was to gather not passive audiences but active preachers and distributors of his materials. "Are you preaching?" asked *Zion's Watch Tower* of July-August, 1881 (p. 241, reprints). "We believe that none will be of the little flock except preachers," was the motivating follow-up to the question. Thus in 1881, when his committed followers numbered only around one hundred, Russell was able to distribute 1,400,000 copies of his tract "Food for Thinking Christians" at the doors of Protestant churches across the United States, Canada, and Britain.

Some expected the movement to fade away when the world failed to end in 1914 as predicted. Russell himself died suddenly two years after the prophetic failure, but his successors Joseph Franklin Rutherford and later Nathan Homer Knorr took the organization Russell left behind and built it into a worldwide publishing empire. From a few thousand *Watch Tower* readers meeting in largely independent, democratically run congregations, the sect has been transformed into a tightly-knit hierarchical organization that controls the lives of 11.5 million people and influences millions more.

2

An Overview

All books and magazines are, of course, expressions of their authors. So the first thing that strikes many readers about recent Jehovah's Witness literature is that no author is listed. Since the early 1940s all literature published by the Watchtower Society has been anonymous, with the rare exception of small personal testimony articles "contributed by" or "as told by" the individual discussed. In fact, the authorship of Watchtower publications is such a closely guarded secret that the few disclosures that have been made public have been revealed by "apostate" ex-Witnesses, persons whom loyal JWs are forbidden to speak to and whose works they are forbidden to read.

But it was not always that way. The sect's founder and first president, Charles Taze Russell, published all of his books and articles in his own name. In fact, it was his personal name that attracted readers and lecture audiences long before the organizational names Watchtower or Jehovah's Witnesses became well known. Commenting on this today the sect's current leadership accuses Russell's followers of "exalting creatures, indulging in a personality cult that focused on Charles T. Russell" (*The Watchtower*, May 1, 1989, p. 4).

Although lacking Russell's charm and wit, his successor, Joseph Franklin ("Judge") Rutherford, likewise published books and articles in his own name. Often characterized as rough and stern compared with his predecessor, he put greater emphasis on "the Society" and "the organization" to secure the organizational loyalty of followers not attracted by his personality. Taking control following Russell's death in 1916, he pledged that "the policies which Brother Russell inaugurated I will attempt to carry forward" (*The Watchtower,* January 15, 1917, p. 6034, reprints). But, in fact, he steered the organization in a different direction altogether, and the literature produced prior to his own death in 1942 bears the distinct stamp of his character.

The third president, Nathan Homer Knorr, was reputed to be more of an administrator than a theologian. In fact, insiders who later defected from the group credit Frederick W. Franz (who eventually became president in 1977) with guiding the organization's doctrinal development during Knorr's administration. But neither Franz's name nor Knorr's appears as author on any Watchtower literature.

Although outsiders may initially see Jehovah's Witness publications as a monolithic library upholding a unique doctrinal perspective, closer inspection reveals considerable fluctuation in belief over the years. Much like a collection of White House news releases written during successive Democratic and Republican administrations, the Watchtower Society's books and magazines reflect the sect's changing leadership over the years. Publications produced under Russell's presidency, for example, contain repeated references to the Great Pyramid of Egypt, promoting it as "God's Stone Witness and Prophet."[1] During the first years of Rutherford's administration, while he was still consolidating power, the teaching remained essentially the same: "The great Pyramid of Egypt, standing as a silent and inanimate witness of the Lord, is a messenger; and its testimony speaks with great eloquence concerning the divine plan."[2] But, after gaining firm control of the organization, Rutherford reversed the teaching, causing *The Watch Tower* to say the exact opposite of what it had been saying only three years earlier. It now identified the Great Pyramid as "Satan's Bible, and not God's stone witness."[3] And it attacked "those who have devoted themselves to the pyramid," accusing them of "being led by vain philosophy and false science and not following after Christ."[4] This completely ignored the fact that "those" had received such teaching from the Watch Tower Society itself over a period of some fifty years.

Perhaps the most violent clash among the leaders responsible for Watchtower literature took place at the beginning of Rutherford's presidency, when he had his helper A. H. Macmillan call the police into the Brooklyn headquarters offices. A policeman "twirling a long night stick around in his hand" was used by Rutherford to forcibly remove Governing Body members who sought to limit his authority—"four of them, which was a majority of the board. There were seven on the board."[5] The result of such tactics was that, although Russell had left behind instructions for a committee to run the organization's publishing operations, Rutherford seized personal control.

Named as a co-defendant in a libel suit brought by a former headquarters staff member, Fred Franz was questioned on the witness stand before the New York supreme court in 1940 as to who "became the Editor of the magazine, the main editor of the 'Watch Tower' magazine?" Fred Franz replied, "Jehovah God." Then, after further questioning produced evasive replies as to the humans responsible for the magazine's contents, the presiding judge asked Franz, "Who had the final say?" He then admitted that "Judge Rutherford supervised everything that went into the magazine, sir."[6]

Following the strongman presidencies of Russell and Rutherford the Watchtower organization began a slow transition toward more collective leadership. Changes in teaching during the successive administrations of Nathan Homer Knorr and Frederick W. Franz often resulted from power struggles among their underlings at Brooklyn headquarters. Thus there was a softening of the sect's stand on several issues during the mid-to-late 1970s while Raymond Franz (President Fred Franz's nephew) and his liberal associates wielded influence and wrote many of the books and magazine articles. But conservatives rallied early in 1980, put several of the liberals on trial before "judicial committees," and expelled them as "apostates."[7] *Time* of February 22, 1982, devoted a full page to the purge after it culminated in the expulsion of Raymond Franz himself (p. 66). This shift in power at the top was reflected by a dramatic reversal in teaching as new Watchtower publications began once again to proclaim views that had been espoused earlier but that were rejected during the liberal period. For example, the September 15, 1981, *Watchtower* reinstituted strict excommunication policies that had been rejected as "extreme"[8] in the August 1, 1974, issue of the same magazine.

One can only guess at the behind-the-scenes political maneuvering at Brooklyn headquarters that caused repeated flip-flops on the question of whether or not the men of Sodom and Gomorrah will be resurrected. The answers given in Watchtower publications are as follows:

1. Yes. *The Watchtower,* July, 1879, p. 8
2. No. *The Watchtower,* June 1, 1952, p. 338
3. Yes. *The Watchtower,* August 1, 1965, p. 479
4. No. *The Watchtower,* June 1, 1988, p. 31
5. Yes. *You Can Live Forever in Paradise on Earth* (1982 edition), p. 179
6. No. *Revelation—Its Grand Climax at Hand!* (1988), p. 273
7. Yes. *Insight on the Scriptures,* vol. 2, 1988, p. 985

8. No. *You Can Live Forever in Paradise on Earth* (1989 revision), p. 179

Introduced in the June 1, 1988, *Watchtower* magazine, the latest reversal evidently caught the press run for *Revelation—Its Grand Climax at Hand!* but missed being incorporated into the more complex *Insight on the Scriptures,* so that Jehovah's Witnesses who received both books at their convention that summer found that their new books contradicted each other. An additional problem surfaced when it was noticed that the 1982 book *You Can Live Forever in Paradise on Earth* (still in daily use as the basic text for indoctrinating new converts) taught the now out-of-favor affirmative answer on this matter of resurrection. So, a revised edition was printed with this doctrine reversed, and Jehovah's Witnesses with existing copies were encouraged to pencil in the change:

> Some adjustments will be made in future printings of the *Live Forever* book. The only significant change is with regard to the Sodomites, on pages 178 and 179. This change appeared in the *Revelation* book, page 273, and in *The Watchtower* of June 1, 1988, pages 30 and 31. You may wish to note it in earlier printings that you have on hand. ("Announcements," *Our Kingdom Ministry,* December 1989, p. 7)

The 11.5 million people who attend JW kingdom halls and who read these publications are taught to view such changes not as the product of shifts in majority opinion at headquarters but as "new light" or "new truths" from God. (This view of the resurrection reversal was facilitated by the fact that the vast majority of Witnesses had converted to or grown up in the organization after 1965, so most were not aware that the *new truth* of 1988 had been taught between 1952 and 1965 until it was rejected then as *error.*) Whenever this sort of reversal occurs, a small number of JWs leave the organization after discovering that their doctrines derive from back-room politics rather than divine revelation; but, since such ones are punished severely with mandatory shunning by family and friends, it is impossible to guess how many others see through the charade but keep silent as did those in the tale of the emperor's new clothes.[9]

In any case, it is important to locate a Watchtower Society book or magazine in its proper organizational and historical setting to understand it and its relationship to Jehovah's Witnesses today and their current beliefs. A change in administration at Watchtower headquarters, or even the passing of a year, can mean an entirely different context. Therefore, this *Guide* groups the literature under the organization's presidents and arranges it chronologically within that grouping.

While this book was in production, fourth Watchtower president Frederick W. Franz passed away at the age of ninety-nine. Franz was the guiding force behind JW literature for some fifty years, from the death of "Judge" Rutherford in 1942 until now. But his longevity protected his doctrine from replacement long after much of it went past its shelf life and began to spoil. Current Watchtower books are filled with details claiming fulfillment of Bible end-times prophecies upon Franz's generation, with only the battle of Armageddon remaining—to occur before that generation passes away.

It had been expected that "the battle of Armageddon will be all over by the autumn of 1975," with a possible "difference of weeks or months, not years" (*The Watchtower,* August 15, 1968, p. 499). But weeks and months have indeed stretched into years, and now Franz, one of the last remaining members of the final "generation" has died. The "Creator's promise of a peaceful and secure new world before the generation that saw the events of 1914 passes away," found on page 4 of each *Awake!* magazine as recently as the issue of April 8, 1993, is obviously overdue for replacement.

Franz was succeeded by long-time vice president Milton G. Henschel. No new books have yet been published under his presidency, but the JWs writing them face the formidable task of leading the sect in a new direction while maintaining some semblance of continuity with the existing volumes of Jehovah's Witness literature catalogued here.

3

The Charles Taze Russell Era
1879–1916

Founder-President
Born February 16, 1852
Died October 31, 1916

Periodicals

Zion's Watch Tower and Herald of Christ's Presence,
renamed in 1909 ***The Watch Tower and Herald of Christ's
Presence***

Our chapter on origins explains that Charles Taze Russell resigned as one of the assistant editors of *The Herald
of the Morning*, an Adventist periodical, and began publishing his own magazine. "In 1879 Charles Taze Russell
began the publication of THE WATCH TOWER, of which
he was the sole editor as long as he remained on earth,"
according to the publisher's preface of *The Finished Mystery* (1917), p. 4. However, examination of the magazine
itself reveals that his wife Maria filled the post of associate
editor for some years, and that "Mrs. Russell's name as Associate Editor first disappeared from the 2nd page of the Tower

in the issue of Nov. 1st, 1896," several years prior to their divorce (*The Watchtower,* July 15, 1906, p. 3812 [reprints]).

Although they feature much of the same material as Russell's books, the magazines often present it in a more personal way and include feedback in the form of testimonies, expressions of appreciation, and questions from readers.

In July 1919, a set of *Watch Tower* reprints was published consolidating articles from the first forty years into seven large volumes, 6,622 pages in all.

Books

Three Worlds, or Plan of Redemption, by Nelson H. Barbour and Charles T. Russell, 1877

Prominently featuring a dispensational chart of the ages, this book develops the Adventist views of biblical chronology, prophecy, and eschatology taught by Second Adventist preacher Nelson H. Barbour of Rochester, New York. The title page says that the book was published by N. H. Barbour and C. T. Russell, with Barbour's name appearing above Russell's and in much larger type. But in the preface by N. H. Barbour he refers to himself as "the writer," and the book itself is written in the singular first person; so, it would appear that Russell shared more in the publication than in the authorship of *Three Worlds.* In fact, in *Zion's Watch Tower* of July 15, 1906, he admits that "it was mainly written by Mr. Barbour" (p. 3822, Society's reprints).

While the subject of deity is not directly discussed, the writer defends the trinitarian view of the Holy Spirit as a person and attacks Christadelphians for deviating from this:

> I am beginning to think Age-to-come people, and many others among pre-millennialists, do not believe in *anything* of a spiritual nature . . . or in the existance [sic] of spiritual beings, or even of the Holy Spirit itself. I *know* one class of age-to-come believers, the *Christadelphians,* do not. The Holy Spirit, say

they, is but a *principle,* or element of power, and not an intelligence. It is nothing more nor less than "electricity," is taught in one of their books, now before me. (pp. 57–58)

There is no record of Russell disputing with Barbour on this point, but five years after the publication of *Three Worlds,* and three years after he left Barbour's company over other issues, Russell devoted several pages of the July 1882 *Watch Tower* to his own arguments against the personality of the Holy Spirit.

Although technically not a Watchtower publication, since it was printed two years before the first issue of the *Watch Tower* magazine, this book is nevertheless listed here because it was copublished by Watchtower founder Charles T. Russell and because it testifies to his affiliation with N. H. Barbour. Prior to breaking away to start his own sect, Charles Russell was assistant editor of the Second Adventist magazine *The Herald of the Morning,* published by Barbour.

Jehovah's Witnesses have been taught to view their religion as totally separate from all the other churches of Christendom, neither related to them nor derived from them, but rather the product of divine intervention. God stepped in, so the Witnesses believe, to restore the truths of first century Christianity through the Watchtower organization. But the publication of *Three Worlds, or Plan of Redemption* by Barbour and Russell in 1877 highlights the fact that the later *Watch Tower* magazine was actually a natural outgrowth of Adventism—a branch of Christendom rather than a separate entity. The Watchtower movement is merely one in a large family of related sects rooted in the dispensationalist school of nineteenth century religious thought.

Although Jehovah's Witnesses today think of Russell as the first in a succession of leaders, earlier Watchtower writings testify to their Adventist roots by presenting Russell as the successor of N. H. Barbour: "Pastor Russell took the place of Mr. Barbour who became unfaithful and upon whom was fulfilled the prophecies of Matt. 24:48–51 and Zech. 11:15–17."[1]

So, although not actually a Watchtower publication in the true sense of the word, *Three Worlds, or Plan of Redemption* deserves mention here, because its very existence reveals the Watchtower sect as a branch of Adventism.

Songs of the Bride, 1879

An advertisement printed on a back page of *Three Worlds* offers the reader

> "SONGS OF THE MORNING": A collection of 67 hymns, in harmony with these views, at ten cents a copy, or one dollar a dozen, *free of postage.*

After he broke from N. H. Barbour's Second Adventist group, C. T. Russell no longer shared all of "these views" with Barbour, so he arranged for a special hymnal to be produced in harmony with his own views. Under the heading "Our New Hymn Book" the third issue of *Zion's Watch Tower* carries this announcement in September 1879:

> We will send as soon as possible to each ZION'S WATCH TOWER subscriber, a copy of *"Songs of the Bride."*
> When you receive it please examine leisurely and carefully. If it does not please you, or if you do not want it, please return it to us. If you like and want to have it, keep it. If you can afford and desire to pay for it, you may do so. (p. 31, reprints)

At this time *Zion's Watch Tower* was being read largely by unsuspecting Christians who accepted the offer of a religious magazine without fully realizing the directions in which its editor was heading. Similarly, when they examined this new hymnal, they would find traditional music sung in many churches. Only if they happened to notice a pattern in the hymns that were omitted would they sense that something was amiss.

Day Dawn, by J. H. Paton, 1880

In 1878, N. H. Barbour's magazine *The Herald of the Morning* listed J. H. Paton of Almont, Michigan, along with C. T. Russell as assistant editors. But Paton soon left the Second Adventists and joined Russell in forming his new breakaway sect. He wrote *Day Dawn* to replace Barbour's *Three Worlds*, and Russell promoted the book. In 1881, however, Russell and Paton split, and Russell began warning *Watch Tower* readers against Paton's book and its subsequent revisions. Soon afterward Russell replaced *Day Dawn* with his own *Millennial Dawn* series, but the chronological calculations of Barbour and Paton remained part of the foundation of Russell's date setting.

Millennial Dawn, by Charles T. Russell, 1886–1904

Millennial Dawn is the original title of a series of six books by Pastor Russell. The series was renamed Studies in the Scriptures shortly after the turn of the century. (See Studies in the Scriptures and individual titles.)

Studies in the Scriptures, by Charles T. Russell, et al., 1886–1917

Originally titled Millennial Dawn, this series of books began with six by Pastor Russell: *The Divine Plan of the Ages* (volume 1, 1886), *The Time Is at Hand* (volume 2, 1889), *Thy Kingdom Come* (volume 3, 1891), *The Day of Vengeance* (later titled *The Battle of Armageddon*, volume 4, 1897), *The At-one-ment Between God and Man* (volume 5, 1899), and *The New Creation* (volume 6, 1904). The series was renamed Studies in the Scriptures shortly after the turn of the century. And in 1917, the year following Russell's death, the Watchtower Society under the new presidency of Joseph F. ("Judge") Rutherford published a controversial seventh volume titled *The Finished Mystery*. (See individual titles.)

Insight into the approach used by the "Bible students" in promoting the Studies can be gained from these words of introduction to volume 1 (1913 edition, p. 4):

> Possibly you may be a member of an Epworth League or Christian Endeavor Society, or of a Baptist Young People's Union, and may be called on for an essay on some Scripture topic. How convenient to select one among these numerous studies (covering almost every topic) and to find therein the appropriate Scriptures cited. Ministers use them thus when composing special sermons and addresses. . . .
>
> We invite Christian people of all denominations to join us in our work of extending these "helping hands" to the rising generation.

From this a reader unfamiliar with the publishing organization would assume that the material was compatible with the beliefs of Baptists and other orthodox Christian ministers—a deceptive introduction indeed.

Note: Each of the seven volumes was reprinted many times over the years. The early Millennial Dawn series featured green cloth covers, and the later Studies in the Scriptures editions featured red cloth covers, some emblazoned with the pagan Egyptian religious symbol of a winged globe. The successive printings were usually done without revision, but in some cases prefatory or appended material was added, deleted, or changed, and in a few rare cases the text of the book itself was altered. Where this is significant, it is noted in the discussion of the respective volume. But the reader doing research in the originals should be aware that page numbers of cited material may vary slightly among the various editions, as may the total number of pages.

The Divine Plan of the Ages, by Charles T. Russell, 1886

Originally titled *The Plan of the Ages*, this book begins the Millennial Dawn, or Studies in the Scriptures, series. It presents Russell's dispensational view of human history, as well as his version of the plan of salvation.

The most eye-catching aspect of this book is the fold-out "Chart of the Ages" featured as a frontispiece. Numerous intersecting arcs, pyramids, and parallel lines are used to divide mankind's history into "dispensations" and "ages." The first dispensation extends from Adam's creation to the flood of Noah's day; the second encompasses the "present evil world" from the flood to the harvest of this world; and the third dispensation, called the Fullness of Times, begins by overlapping the second and extends into the indefinite future. The chart further divides the second dispensation into three ages: the patriarchal age, the Jewish age (culminating in a harvest period), and the gospel age (also culminating in a harvest). The third dispensation is likewise divided into the millennial age and ages to come. Further complicating the chart, each harvest period is divided by a number of intersecting arcs, and the termination points of the arcs lead to lines that drop vertically to intersect with parallel "planes," which in turn intersect several pyramids. At the right-hand side of the chart the parallel planes terminate in a sketch of the ancient Jewish tabernacle of the wilderness. Russell devotes a twenty-five page chapter exclusively to explaining the chart. But in this volume he limits himself largely to generalities. In later volumes he looks more closely at the harvest periods, assigning prophetic events to specific dates in the late 1800s and early 1900s.

The Time Is at Hand, by Charles T. Russell, 1889

Volume 2 of the Millennial Dawn, or Studies in the Scriptures, series, this book focuses almost entirely on chronology. It claims parallels between the harvest of the Jewish age (A.D. 29 to A.D. 70) and the harvest of the gospel age (A.D. 1874 to A.D. 1915). These supposed parallels are used to argue that Christ returned invisibly in 1874 and began exercising kingdom power in 1878, that the heavenly calling terminated in 1881, and that "'the battle of the

great day of God Almighty' (Rev. 16:14), which will end in
A.D. 1914 with the complete overthrow of earth's present
rulership, is already commenced" (p. 101, 1904 edition;
date changed to 1915 in some later printings). And the
Roman destruction of the Jewish state in A.D. 70 is presented as pointing to the "entire destruction of nominal
Christendom" in A.D. 1914 (p. 247).

This volume of the Studies also claims the Bible foretold "an Advent Movement in 1844, thirty years prior to
the actual time of His presence, to awaken and test the
Church" (p. 247), that is, the great disappointment of those
who joined William Miller in expecting the return of Christ
in 1844 (p. 240).

Russell also uses this volume to spell out some of the
differences that had developed between himself and the
Second Adventists, the sect he had been fellowshipping
with until some ten years prior to this writing (pp. 243–244):

> It will be noticed by those at all familiar with the calculations
> usually made by "Second Adventists" and others, relative to
> the prophetic periods, etc., that this method of dealing with
> these subjects is very different from theirs. They usually
> attempt to make all prophecies end at some *one* date. Their
> erroneous expectations lead them to this. . . . To appreciate and
> accept the prophecies which point out various dates for vari-
> ous steps in God's great plan, they would need first to under-
> stand the "Plan of the Ages" and the true manner of the Lord's
> second advent. But the great majority are too much blinded by
> their theories and prejudices to do this.

Poems and Hymns of Millennial Dawn, 1890

Replacing *Songs of the Bride* issued eleven years earlier, this volume features 151 poems and 333 hymns, all
printed without music. Like the earlier songbook, this one
contains traditional pieces of music found in many
churches, but it also adds a few hymns written by Russellites themselves. *Zion's Watch Tower* of February 15, 1896,
characterizes it as "not only choice doctrinally, but also
choice poetically" (p. 26). Successive songbooks produced

over the years reflect the organization's ever widening departure from orthodoxy.

Thy Kingdom Come, by Charles T. Russell, 1891
Volume 3 of the Millennial Dawn, or Studies in the Scriptures, series, this book highlights the influence of pyramidology on Watchtower teachings. Prominently featured facing the title page is an illustration captioned, "Vertical Section (from South to North looking West) of the Great Pyramid of Jeezeh," showing such internal passages of the Egyptian monument as the king's chamber, the queen's chamber, the grand gallery, and the grotto—all of which Russell interprets as prophetic regarding the church. The sixty-three-page-long tenth chapter develops these prophecies and is titled, "The Testimony of God's Stone Witness and Prophet, the Great Pyramid in Egypt." This excerpt from page 342 (1903 edition) gives the flavor of this chapter and shows how Russell used the Great Pyramid to arrive at prophetic dates:

> Then measuring *down* the "Entrance Passage" from that point, to find the distance to the entrance of the "Pit," representing the great trouble and destruction with which this age is to close, when evil will be overthrown from power, we find it to be 3416 inches, symbolizing 3416 years from the above date, B.C. 1542. This calculation shows A.D. 1874 as marking the beginning of the period of trouble; for 1542 years B.C. plus 1874 years A.D. equals 3416 years. Thus the Pyramid witnesses that the close of 1874 was the *chronological* beginning of the time of trouble such as was not since there was a nation—no, nor ever shall be afterward.

When he changed his mind on prophetic dates, Russell also changed later editions to read as follows:

> Then measuring *down* the "Entrance Passage" from that point, to find the distance to the entrance of the "Pit," representing the great trouble and destruction with which this age is to close, when evil will be overthrown from power, we find it to be 3457 inches, symbolizing 3457 years from the above date,

B.C. 1542. This calculation shows A.D. 1915 as marking the beginning of the period of trouble; for 1542 years B.C. plus 1915 years A.D. equals 3457 years. Thus the Pyramid witnesses that the close of 1914 will be the beginning of the time of trouble such as was not since there was a nation—no, nor ever shall be afterward.

Notice that he stretched the Pyramid passage by several inches to make it fit his new dating system. This is reminiscent of the words Russell directed at the Second Adventists on page 244 of Studies in the Scriptures, volume 2, where he wrote:

Their attempts to apply prophecy to their false expectations often lead to twisting, stretching or whittling, according to the necessities of the case, in the endeavor to get all the prophecies to terminate at some one date. These friends should awake to their error in this direction; for one after another their expectations have failed, while we and they know that some of the prophecies they have used cannot be stretched into the future, but are in the past, and are now abandoned by them.

Not long after hurling this criticism at the Second Adventists, Russell himself had to stretch not only his prophecies but also the measurements of the Pyramid's stone passage. Moreover, his followers have long since abandoned the Pyramid prophecies entirely, after they had dominated Watchtower thinking for some fifty years.

Another teaching found here in volume 3 that was repeated in other publications and not repudiated until 1953 (November 15th *Watchtower*, p. 703) is the declaration that God resides on the star Alcyone in the Pleiades constellation. Here an authority is quoted who speaks of "Alcyone, the central one of the renowned Pleiadic stars ... from which the Almighty governs his universe" (p. 327). For more on the Pleiades, see also *Reconciliation* (1928).

Joseph B. Rotherham's New Testament (12th edition, revised), 1896

The Pennsylvania corporation formed in 1884 as Zion's Watch Tower Tract Society was renamed in 1896. It became the Watch Tower Bible & Tract Society, and it published its first Bible in that year. Printing rights were obtained from British translator Joseph B. Rotherham to publish in the United States the twelfth edition (revised) of his *New Testament.*

The Day of Vengeance or *The Battle of Armageddon*, by Charles T. Russell, 1897

Originally titled *The Day of Vengeance* but later renamed *The Battle of Armageddon,* this book constitutes volume 4 of the Millennial Dawn, or Studies in the Scriptures, series. At great length it attempts to draw parallels between Christendom and ancient Babylon of the prophet Daniel's day. Its conclusion is that Christendom deserves destruction, that mankind has no viable substitute to offer, and that ultimately God will destroy Christendom and replace it with his kingdom ruling over the earth.

Since this volume of Studies in the Scriptures contains little in the way of the prophetic date setting that characterizes certain other volumes, it is seldom referred to today by critics of the Watchtower Society. And the Society itself has long since shelved the entire series, even removing the books from local kingdom hall libraries so that Jehovah's Witnesses will not read them.

The At-one-ment Between God and Man, by Charles T. Russell, 1899

(*Note*: Some editions of this book, such as that of 1913, were printed with the 128-page *Tabernacle Shadows* booklet appended to the volume, although not noted on the cover. Please see our separate discussion of *Tabernacle Shadows*.)

Volume 5 of the Millennial Dawn, or Studies in the Scriptures, series, this book is significant in that it provides an extensive and detailed presentation of C. T. Russell's nontrinitarian theology. Nearly the first half of the book is devoted to discussion of the person of God the Father, the person of Jesus Christ, and the role of the Holy Spirit.

Jesus is said to have "existed as a spirit being before he was made flesh and dwelt amongst men," but he is described as "a god," the "highest angel," and "the first, the direct creation of God" (p. 92 in the edition of 1899; p. 84 in certain later editions). And "the prevalent thought that the holy Spirit is a person" is called a "misconception." Russell presents the Holy Spirit instead as "merely the divine spirit, influence or power" (p. 187 in the edition of 1899; p. 172 in certain later editions).

Zion's Glad Songs, 1900

Later referred to as "the musical TOWER," the February 1, 1896, issue of *Zion's Watch Tower* consists almost entirely of eleven new hymns by M. L. McPhail under the collective title of *Zion's Glad Songs of the Morning*. Back copies of "the musical TOWER" were used as supplements to the 1890 hymnal until 1900, when this paperbound book of eighty-two songs, mostly by McPhail, was released in a first edition of six thousand copies. *Zion's Glad Songs* thereafter supplemented *Poems and Hymns of Millennial Dawn* at Russellite meetings.

Holman Linear Bible, 1902

This volume presents the Authorized and Revised versions of the Old and New Testaments as a single line of large type where they read the same, and as a double line of small type where there are differences in wording. A wide margin features explanatory notes and references to the Millennial Dawn volumes and *Zion's Watch Tower.*

Poems of Dawn, 1902

This book included the poems only from the 1890 *Poems and Hymns of Millennial Dawn.* A larger edition by the same title was produced in 1912.

The Emphatic Diaglott, by Benjamin Wilson, 1902

In 1902 the Watch Tower Society became copyright owner and sole publisher and distributor of the interlinear translation titled *The Emphatic Diaglott,* concerning which the Society said:

> This had first been published by its author, Benjamin Wilson, a newspaper editor of Geneva, Illinois, in 1864, and who was never associated with the Watch Tower Bible & Tract Society. (*Jehovah's Witnesses in the Divine Purpose,* p. 256)

The Society does not here give Benjamin Wilson's religious affiliation, but *Awake!* magazine's predecessor, *Consolation,* reports that he was a Christadelphian (November 8, 1944, p. 26). Other sources[2] identify him as a member of the Church of God (Faith of Abraham).

Elsewhere the Watchtower Society has admitted the role Benjamin Wilson played in determining certain doctrines of the Second Adventist group headed by N. H. Barbour that Charles Taze Russell was associated with—doctrines that Russell took with him when he left that group to start his own magazine.

> It seems that one of Barbour's group had come into possession of Benjamin Wilson's *Diaglott* translation of the "New Testament." He noticed, at Matthew 24:27, 37, 39, that the word rendered *coming* in the *King James Version* is translated *presence* in the *Diaglott.* This was the clue that had led Barbour's group to advocate, in addition to their time calculations, an invisible presence of Christ. (*Jehovah's Witnesses in the Divine Purpose,* p. 18)

So, when Russell started his own religious magazine in 1879 and called it *Zion's Watch Tower and Herald of Christ's Presence,* this idea of Christ's invisible "presence" was a notion he borrowed from the Second Adventists, who in turn derived it from Benjamin Wilson's writings.

Another prominent Watchtower teaching found earlier in Wilson's work is the description of Jesus Christ as "a god." Although Wilson translates John 1:1 to say "the LOGOS was God," he writes in his interlinear portion, "a god was the Word."

Similarly, in the *Diaglott's* alphabetic appendix Wilson writes that *hades* is "improperly translated" as *hell,* and that *gehenna* "symbolizes *death* and *utter destruction,* but in no place signifies a place of eternal torment" (pp. 891–892).

The New Creation, by Charles T. Russell, 1904

Volume 6 of Millennial Dawn, or Studies in the Scriptures, and the last of the series actually written by Charles T. Russell, this book of more than seven hundred pages concludes the series as far as true Russellites are concerned. Groups loyal to the memory of Pastor Russell such as the Dawn Bible Students, the Chicago Bible Students, and the Laymen's Home Missionary Movement still distribute reprints of volumes 1 through 6 and use them for religious instruction.

Volume 6 focuses on the true church, as Russell saw it, the body of Christ. In this teaching he is much closer to orthodox Christian thought and does not deviate nearly as far as the Jehovah's Witnesses of today. It was Russell's successor J. F. Rutherford who consigned the "great multitude" or "great crowd" of Revelation 7:9 to everlasting life on earth apart from Christ. So when Jehovah's Witnesses now express their belief that, of the 10 million currently attending their kingdom halls, fewer than nine thousand will go to heaven, they owe this teaching to Rutherford, not Russell. *The New Creation* presents the "great company" as made up of "the Lord's truly consecrated people" who "let slip their opportunity for becoming members of the Bride" (p. 127) but still go to heaven as a secondary spiritual class.

Hymns of the Millennial Dawn, 1905–1906

Dated and copyrighted in 1905 but not actually released until April 1906, this songbook features the same

333 hymns published in 1890, with the addition of music and with some changes in the lyrics. According to *Jehovah's Witnesses in the Divine Purpose* the words of familiar old hymns "were changed only to delete doctrinal error as found in the denominational church systems from which they were borrowed" (p. 259). Revised hymnals were also produced in 1909 and 1916.

Daily Heavenly Manna for the Household of Faith, by Gertrude W. Seibert, 1907

With a Bible text for each day of the year, this is the precursor of the Watchtower Society's later *Yearbooks*. Originally published privately by its author in 1905, the book came to be distributed by the Society and was used in

> morning religious devotions and especially at the Wednesday night prayer, praise and testimony meetings. The book was used for keeping a record of birthdays and collecting signatures and addresses of fellow Bible students. (*"Then is Finished The Mystery of God,"* pp. 145–146)

In 1927 the *Manna* book was replaced by a *Yearbook* prepared by the Watchtower's male writing staff, as it was no longer deemed appropriate for the organization to distribute a book written by a woman.

Berean Bible, 1907

Named after the Bereans referred to in Acts 17:11, this is a King James Version of the Bible published by the Watchtower Society in 1907, with a one-hundred-page concordance and more than six hundred pages of notes.

Bible Student's Manual, by Clayton J. Woodworth, 1909

In 482 pages this *Manual* lists nearly every verse in the Bible, from Genesis to Revelation, referring the reader to explanatory material by Pastor Russell. References are to Studies in the Scriptures and *Zion's Watch Tower* primarily, but also to booklets, articles, and even newspaper reports of sermons Russell delivered. Thus equipped, a Russellite reading the Bible could find the pastor's explanation of virtually any verse he might come upon. Today's equivalent is the 169-page by five-columns-wide Scripture index in the *Watch Tower Publications Index 1930–1985,* plus yearly supplements.

Poems of Dawn, 1912

Omitted when the hymns alone from the 1890 *Poems and Hymns of Millennial Dawn* were reprinted with music in 1906, the poems were printed as a separate volume in 1912. This volume was nearly a hundred pages longer than the 1902 edition by the same title.

Scenario of the Photo-Drama of Creation, by Charles T. Russell, 1914

The Photo-Drama of Creation was an eight-hour-long presentation of colored slides and motion pictures, synchronized with phonograph records, that Russell began producing in 1912. Ahead of its time—motion pictures with sound did not appear commercially until the next decade—the Photo-Drama drew huge audiences around the world. What they saw and heard was a combination of science, world history, and Russell's interpretation of biblical chronology. This spectacular production led thousands to Russell and his works.

The *Scenario of the Photo-Drama of Creation* is a 192-page printed version with sepia prints of many of the slides, accompanied by the text of ninety-six "short lectures." Introductory material opposite the title page states that "the Drama is unsectarian and inter-denominational."

Pastor Russell's Sermons, 1917

Described on its title page as "a choice collection of his most important discourses on all phases of Christian doctrine and practise," this volume of more than eight hundred pages was published shortly after Russell's death. When Jehovah's Witnesses see Peoples Pulpit Association listed as the publisher and neither Watch Tower Bible and Tract Society nor International Bible Students Association mentioned on the title page, they sometimes conclude that this volume must have been published by one of the Russellite groups that broke away from Judge Rutherford's control. However, that is not the case. People's Pulpit Association was the original designation of the Watchtower Bible and Tract Society of New York, Inc., when C. T. Russell founded it as a branch operation in 1909. So, *Pastor Russell's Sermons* is a Watch Tower publication as much so as any other. But, while Jehovah's Witnesses seldom see a copy and treat it as a suspicious relic of the past if they do run across it, the Russellites do reprint it today and read it as instructional material.

The Finished Mystery

Although this seventh volume of Studies in the Scriptures is presented as the posthumous work of C. T. Russell, it actually belongs in the Rutherford era and is discussed there.

Booklets

Watchtower booklets are simply listed here. Only those of lasting significance are discussed.

The Object and Manner of Our Lord's Return, by Charles T. Russell, (1873 [?] or 1877)

Actually a pre-Watchtower publication dated prior to the first *Zion's Watch Tower* magazine, this booklet teaches that Christ returns invisibly in a spiritual body.

Although the Watchtower Society now says Russell self-published the booklet in 1873,[3] the only extant copies we know of have the date 1877 on the title page under the heading, "Rochester, N.Y.: Office of Herald of the Morning." Moreover, the copy we have seen makes reference on page 51 to *The Emphatic Diaglott*'s translation of *parousia* as Christ's "presence" rather than "coming"—a piece of information that the Society indicates Russell learned from Nelson Barbour in 1876 (*Jehovah's Witnesses in the Divine Purpose,* p. 18). So, if there was, in fact, an 1873 printing of this booklet, it must have undergone major revision in 1877.

Food for Thinking Christians, by Charles T. Russell, 1881

Appearing first as a special September 1881 issue of *Zion's Watch Tower,* this was reprinted in booklet form. Today, in fact, we would call it a small book. *Food for Thinking Christians* focuses primarily on the return of Christ and the resurrection, using a dispensational chart of the ages to link end-times events mathematically with prior events from the Bible record. But, to capture the reader's attention, the booklet features on its title page the subtitle *Why Evil Was Permitted* and begins with a dialogue on that subject. It also features an attack on spiritualism. The booklet could be considered an outline for much of what Russell would later develop in considerably greater detail in his Studies in the Scriptures. Between 1881 and 1885 more than a million copies of *Food for Thinking Christians* were distributed, including hundreds of thousands sent free to the entire subscription lists of certain major newspapers in New York, Chicago, Boston, and Philadelphia.

The Tabernacle and Its Teachings, by Charles T. Russell, 1881

Along with *Food for Thinking Christians* this large booklet was distributed free to thousands of worshipers in the United States and England as they exited Protestant churches following Sunday morning services. This booklet was revised and retitled *Tabernacle Shadows of the "Better Sacrifices."*

Tabernacle Shadows of the "Better Sacrifices," by Charles T. Russell, 1881 (a revision of *The Tabernacle and Its Teachings*)

Note: This booklet can also be found as a 128-page appendix to certain editions of the book *At-one-ment Between God and Man,* volume 5 of Studies in the Scriptures.

Taking its cue from the New Testament Letter to the Hebrews this booklet goes far beyond what is written in Hebrews in deriving prophetic illustrations from the ancient Jewish tabernacle of worship.

Outlines of Sermons, by Charles T. Russell, 1882

The May 1882 *Watch Tower* announced the availability of outlines for six sermons that would enable readers to explain the chart of the ages to others. Since readers were encouraged to hang the chart on a prominent wall in their homes, there would presumably be many opportunities to use the outlines in explaining the chart.

The Wonderful Story, by Charles T. Russell, 1890

The Divine Plan of the Ages for Human Salvation (An Epitomized Statement of the Divine Plan of the Ages), by Charles T. Russell, 1892

"Thy Word Is Truth"—An Answer to Robert Ingersoll's Charges Against Christianity, by Charles T. Russell, 1892

Zion's Watch Tower and Herald of Christ's Presence (Extra Edition)—A Conspiracy Exposed: Harvest Siftings, by Charles T. Russell, 1894

This special issue of the *Watch Tower* in the form of a brochure or booklet attacks certain individuals who challenged Russell's character and authority. Naturally, only Russell's side of the dispute is presented, but it does shed some light on the nature of internal dissention in the organization he founded.

This publication is not to be confused with the *Harvest Siftings* produced by J. F. Rutherford in 1917 during the factional infighting that followed Russell's death.

What Say the Scriptures About Hell? by Charles T. Russell, 1895

This, perhaps more than any other Watch Tower publication, gained Pastor Russell his reputation as the man who "turned the hose on hell."

Outlines of the Divine Plan of the Ages, by Charles T. Russell, 1896

What Say the Scriptures About Spiritualism (Spiritism)? by Charles T. Russell, 1897

The Bible Versus the Evolution Theory, by Charles T. Russell, 1898

What Say the Scriptures About Our Lord's Return? by Charles T. Russell, 1898

Tabernacle Shadows, by Charles T. Russell, 1899

Souvenir. (notes from) Watch Tower Bible and Tract Society's Conventions, 1905

Between 1904 and 1969 dozens of souvenir convention reports were published in connection with the sect's large gatherings, but only those of 1905 and 1963 are listed here. Filled with artists' drawings and photographs of ordinary members and Watchtower dignitaries, the convention reports advertised new publications released at these assemblies, documented their international flavor, and reported on the programs presented.

Instructor's Guide and Berean Index, 1907

The Sin-Offering and the Covenants, by Charles T. Russell, 1909

Berean Studies on The At-one-ment Between God and Man, 1910

Jewish Hopes, by Charles T. Russell, 1910

Berean Studies on The Divine Plan of The Ages, 1911

Questions on "Tabernacle Studies," 1911

Berean Studies on The Battle of Armageddon, 1912

Berean Studies on The Time Is At Hand, 1912

Berean Studies on Thy Kingdom Come, 1912

Berean Studies on The New Creation, 1914

A Great Battle in the Ecclesiastical Heavens, by Joseph F. Rutherford, 1915

By the year 1915 Charles Russell was under attack on many fronts, not only for his doctrine, but also in regard to the conduct of his ministry and his personal life. The Society's vice president, J. F. Rutherford, a lawyer by profession, came to Russell's defense in this booklet. An announcement by Russell in the May 1, 1915, *Watch Tower* is titled, "Judge Rutherford's Spicy Defense," and says:

> Brother Rutherford, grieved by the various untruthful, slanderous attacks upon the Editor, has prepared a pamphlet in my defense. A copy of it has just been handed me. I have not yet read it, though, of course, I knew of its preparation and in a general way of its contents. I prefer not to have anything to do with its publication. It explains Brother Rutherford's views as a lawyer, as a brother, and as a man who most fully understands the entire situation. . . .
>
> Orders for the pamphlets should be addressed to Judge Rutherford, New York City, P.O. Box 51. However, we will have a supply at THE WATCH TOWER Office, and, if one is ordering other things, this pamphlet can be supplied also. (p. 5685 [Society's reprints])

An Index to the Towers From January 1st, 1908 to October 15, 1915, 1916

Tracts and Pamphlets

Watchtower tracts and pamphlets are almost too numerous to mention. They are simply listed here. Only those of lasting significance are discussed.

Bible Students' Tract No. 1, 1881

Bible Students' Tract No.2, 1881

Bible Students' Tract No. 3, 1881

Bible Students' Tract No. 4: Why Evil Was Permitted, 1881

Bible Students' Tract No. 5: The Narrow Way to Life, 1881

Arp Slips (also called *Arp Tracts*), 1887

The Old Theology, No. 1: Do the Scriptures Teach That Eternal Torment Is the Wages of Sin? 1889

The Old Theology, No. 2: The Scripture Teaching on Calamities, and Why God Permits Them, 1889

The Old Theology, No. 3: Protestants Awake! 1889

The Old Theology, No. 4: Dr. Talmage's View of the Millennium, 1889

The Old Theology, No. 5: Friendly Hints on Bible Study and Students' Helps, 1889

The Old Theology, No. 6: The Scripture Teaching Concerning the World's Hope, 1889

The Old Theology, No. 7: The Wonderful Story of Wisdom, Love and Grace Divine, 1889

The Old Theology, No. 8 (an illustrated version of No. 7), 1889

The Old Theology, No. 9 (a Swedish translation of No. 1), 1889

The Old Theology, No. 10: Contend Earnestly for the Faith Once Delivered to the Saints, 1889

The Old Theology, No. 11: The Tabernacle Shadows of the "Better Sacrifices," 1889

Old Theology Quarterly, No. 12: The Divine Plan of the Ages for Human Salvation—Why Evil Was Permitted, 1892

Old Theology Quarterly, No. 13 (a Norwegian translation of No. 1), 1892

Old Theology Quarterly, No. 14: A Dark Cloud and its Silver Lining, 1892

Old Theology Quarterly, No. 15: "Thy Word Is Truth"— An Answer to Robert Ingersoll's Charges Against Christianity, 1892

Old Theology Quarterly, No. 16 (the text of No. 15 in booklet form), 1892

Old Theology Quarterly, No. 17: The Scripture Teaching on Purgatory, 1892

Old Theology Quarterly, No. 18: Representative or Substitute? 1892

Old Theology Quarterly, No. 19 (a Norwegian translation of No. 14), 1892

Old Theology Quarterly, No. 20 (a Swedish translation of No. 14), 1892

Old Theology Quarterly, No. 21: Do You Know? 1892

Old Theology Quarterly, No. 22 (a new edition of No. 6), 1892

Old Theology Quarterly, No. 23 (a German translation of No. 21), 1892

Old Theology Quarterly, No. 24 (a new edition of No. 5), 1892

Old Theology Quarterly, No. 25: The Only Name—A Criticism of Bishop Fonter's New Gospel, 1892

Old Theology Quarterly, No. 26 (a Swedish translation of No. 21), 1892

Old Theology Quarterly, No. 27 (a new edition of No. 14), 1892

Old Theology Quarterly, No. 28: Why Are Ye Last to Welcome Back the King? 1892

Old Theology Quarterly, No. 29 (a Norwegian translation of No. 21), 1892

Old Theology Quarterly, No. 30 (a German translation of No. 28), 1892

Old Theology Quarterly, No. 30 extra: Wait Thou Upon the Lord, 1892

Old Theology Quarterly, No. 31: A Helping Hand for Bible Students (an advertisement for the Millennial Dawn books), 1892

Old Theology Quarterly, No. 32: What Say the Scriptures About Hell? 1892

Old Theology Quarterly, No. 33 (a Dutch translation of No. 1), 1892

Old Theology Quarterly, No. 34 (a German translation of No. 1), 1892

Old Theology Quarterly, No. 35 (a Swedish translation of No. 28), 1892

Old Theology Quarterly, No. 35 extra (a French translation of No. 21), 1892

Old Theology Quarterly, No. 36: Awake! Jerusalem, Awake! 1892

Old Theology Quarterly, No. 37: "How Readest Thou?" 1892

Old Theology Quarterly, No. 38: The Hope of Immortality, 1892

Old Theology Quarterly, No. 39: What Say the Scriptures About Spiritualism? 1892

Old Theology Quarterly, No. 40: What Is the Soul? 1892

Old Theology Quarterly, No. 41: Must We Abandon Hope of a Golden Age? 1892

Old Theology Quarterly, No. 42: Crucified With Christ, 1892

Old Theology Quarterly, No. 43: The Bible Versus the Evolution Theory, 1892

Old Theology Quarterly, No. 44: Gathering the Lord's Jewels, 1892

Old Theology Quarterly, No. 45 (a new edition of No. 8), 1892

Old Theology Quarterly, No. 46: The Good Shepherd and His Two Flocks, 1892

Old Theology Quarterly, No. 47 (a Swedish translation of No. 40), 1892

Old Theology Quarterly, No. 48: What Say the Scriptures About Our Lord's Return? 1892

Old Theology Quarterly, No. 49: Which Is the True Gospel? 1892

Old Theology Quarterly, No. 50 (a German translation of No. 49), 1892

Old Theology Quarterly, No. 51 (a new edition of No. 30 extra), 1892

Old Theology Quarterly, No. 52: Our Lord's Return, Its Object, the Restitution of All Things Spoken, 1892

Old Theology Quarterly, No. 53 (a new edition of No. 1), 1892

Old Theology Quarterly, No. 54 (a new edition of No. 14), 1892

Old Theology Quarterly, No. 55 (a new edition of No. 32), 1892

Old Theology Quarterly, No. 56 (none extant, no record of the title), 1892

Old Theology Quarterly, No. 57 (a new edition of No. 2), 1892

Old Theology Quarterly, No. 58 (a new edition of No. 17), 1892

Old Theology Quarterly, No. 59 (a new edition of No. 6), 1892

Old Theology Quarterly, No. 60 (a new edition of No. 28), 1892

Old Theology Quarterly, No. 61 (a new edition of No. 3), 1892

Old Theology Quarterly, No. 62 (a new edition of No. 12), 1892

Old Theology Quarterly, No. 63: Christ's Death Secured, 1892

Old Theology Quarterly, No. 64: Criticisms of Millennial Hopes and Prospects Examined, 1892

Old Theology Quarterly, No. 65 (a new edition of No. 11), 1892

Old Theology Quarterly, No. 66 (a new edition of No. 21), 1892

Old Theology Quarterly, No. 67 (none extant, no record of the title), 1892

Old Theology Quarterly, No. 68: Increasing Influence of Spiritism, 1892

Old Theology Quarterly, No. 69: Study to Show Thyself Approved Unto God. Christendom in Grave Danger. Refrain Thy Voice From Weeping. Hope for the Innumerable Non-Elect, 1892

Old Theology Quarterly, No. 70: Cheerful Christians. Divine Predestination in Respect to Mankind, 1892

Old Theology Quarterly, No. 71 (a new edition of No. 15), 1892

Old Theology Quarterly, No 72: To Hell and Back! Who Are There. The Great Prison House to be Destroyed. The Oath-Bound Covenant. Selling the Birthright (a new edition of No. 1), 1892

Old Theology Quarterly, No. 73 (a new edition of No. 2), 1892

Old Theology Quarterly, No. 74 (a new edition of No. 12), 1892

Old Theology Quarterly, No. 75: Spiritism is Demonism, 1892

Old Theology Quarterly, No. 76: Earthquakes in Prophecy. Tongues of Fire. "In the Evil Day." Filthiness of Flesh and Spirit, 1892

Old Theology Quarterly, No. 77 (none extant; no record of title), 1892

Old Theology Quarterly, No. 78 (a new edition of No. 48), 1892

Old Theology Quarterly, No. 79 (none extant; no record of title), 1892

Old Theology Quarterly, No. 80: Are You of the Hopeful or of the Hopeless? Seven Women Desire One Husband.

The Millennial Morning Is Dawning! The Ransom Price Paid for Sinners Guarantees a Millennial Age of Restitution, 1892

People's Pulpit tracts (later titled *Everybody's Paper*, and then *The Bible Students Monthly*), 1909

These eye-appealing tracts featuring cartoons and other illustrations were published monthly beginning in 1909. Volunteers distributed millions of them by slipping them under the doors of homes and by handing them to people filing out of churches after Sunday morning services.

Charles Taze Russell died on board a Santa Fe Railroad train while passing through Pampa, Texas, on October 31, 1916. Thus ended his control over the writing and publishing of Watchtower literature, but his articles continued to be reprinted in *The Watch Tower,* and his books continued to be reprinted by the Society for many years and were distributed by Jehovah's Witnesses until at least 1967.

JWs usually dispute this, because the Society's anonymously written 1973 book *God's Kingdom of a Thousand Years Has Approached* tells them that "later in the year 1927 any remaining stocks of the six volumes of Studies in the Scriptures by Russell and of *The Finished Mystery* were disposed of among the public" (p. 347). However *The Bulletin* of December 1, 1932, proclaims that over 100,000 copies of Studies in the Scriptures were sold during 1931 (p.1). The Watchtower publications *Cost List,* provided to men selling books at kingdom hall book rooms, shows Studies in the Scriptures as still being offered in February of 1944 (pp. 1, 6). And the *Kingdom Ministry* of July 1967 includes in its listing of changes in availability of literature the announcement that Studies in the Scriptures, vol. 4, has gone out of stock in the United States (p. 3).

4

The Joseph F. Rutherford Era
1917–1942

President
Born November 8, 1869
Died January 8, 1942

Periodicals

The Watch Tower and Herald of Christ's Presence, renamed *The Watchtower and Herald of Christ's Presence* in 1931, *The Watchtower and Herald of Christ's Kingdom* on January 1, 1939, and *The Watchtower Announcing Jehovah's Kingdom* on March 1, 1939, the title as of this writing

In July 1919, a set of *Watch Tower* reprints was published consolidating articles from the first forty years into seven large volumes, 6,622 pages in all.

It is significant that the magazine's name was changed during Rutherford's administration from one proclaiming "Christ's Presence" to one announcing "Jehovah's Kingdom." The same period saw a change in doctrinal emphasis from concentration on Christ (albeit heretically) to focus on the Father, with the new stress on the name *Jehovah* that hinted at a gradual Judaizing of the sect. And rather than the King, Rutherford put the kingdom to the forefront, with the Watchtower organization presented as the visible earthly manifestation of God's kingdom.

For a selection of approximately one hundred *Watchtower* magazine quotations that trace these and other doctrinal changes through the Rutherford era, please see my book *Index of Watchtower Errors* (Baker Book House, 1990).

The Golden Age, first published on October 1, 1919; renamed **Consolation** in 1937 and **Awake!** in 1946

Offered from door to door along with *The Watchtower*, this new magazine featured articles on nonbiblical subjects to draw the interest of nonreligious people.

Bulletin, first published in 1917; renamed **Director** in 1935 and **Informant** in 1936; later renamed **Kingdom Ministry** (1956), **Our Kingdom Service** (1976), then **Our Kingdom Ministry** (1982)

This members-only monthly publication features instructions for carrying on the house-to-house ministry, as well as news about the organization's conventions and new publications.

Books

Pastor Russell's Sermons, by Charles T. Russell, 1917

Although published during the first few months of Rutherford's administration, this volume consists entirely of C. T. Russell's words, and is therefore discussed in our previous chapter.

The Finished Mystery, purportedly the "posthumous work of Pastor Russell" but actually written by Clayton J. Woodworth and George H. Fisher, 1917

Nearly six hundred pages long, *The Finished Mystery* is a verse-by-verse commentary on the Bible books of Revelation, Song of Solomon, and Ezekiel.

Although Charles Taze Russell himself was a controversial man, and his books provoked considerable discussion, *The Finished Mystery* was to that earlier controversy like a hurricane to a spring breeze. This seventh volume of Studies in the Scriptures tore apart the Watchtower organization, splitting it into sectarian groups that still do battle with each other three-quarters of a century later. And it provoked such anger on the part of the United States government that Rutherford and his associates found themselves thrown into federal prison with twenty-year sentences.

Even Jehovah's Witness publications, which seldom reveal anything at all about internal difficulties, tell of a hostile reception from many headquarters workers when the book was released to them at a meal in the Brooklyn Bethel dining room. It had been prepared and published at J. F. Rutherford's command, without the consent or even the knowledge of the majority of the society's board of directors. The book became a major bone of contention between supporters of Rutherford and opponents who eventually split from the Watchtower. To this day a single question is sufficient to determine whether an individual is a Jehovah's Witness or a member of one of the Russellite "Bible Student" sects. Ask how many volumes make up Studies in the Scriptures. A JW will answer seven, whereas a member of one of the breakaway groups will insist there are only six. The latter accept only the volumes written and published by Russell himself. They flatly reject the seventh volume commissioned by Rutherford.

This may seem strange to the uninitiated reader, since *The Finished Mystery* praises Russell exceedingly, classing him as a special messenger to the church on a par with John Wycliffe, Martin Luther, and the apostles Paul and John (pp. 23, 45). But it is not uncommon for competing heirs to an empire to outdo one another in praising the recently deceased leader so as to appear to have his blessing. Russellite Bible Students see Rutherford's praise for Russell as a mere device to gain followers for himself.

The Finished Mystery actually goes beyond praise; it claims Rutherford's presidency and administration to be under the controlling influence of Russell's departed spirit or ghost. In commenting on Revelation 8:3 it says: "This verse shows that, though Pastor Russell has passed beyond the veil, he is still managing every feature of the Harvest work" (p. 144). And later it adds: ". . . we hold that he supervises, by the Lord's arrangement, the work yet to be done" (p. 256). This thought that Russell was still directing the organization from beyond the grave is also reflected in the November 1, 1917, *Watch Tower* magazine: "Hence our dear Pastor, now in glory, is without doubt, manifesting a keen interest in the harvest work, and is permitted by the Lord to exercise some strong influence thereupon" (p. 6161 [Society's reprints]). This teaching remained in effect until it was repudiated in Rutherford's 1934 book *Jehovah* (see discussion).

Perhaps not surprisingly, Rutherford's opponents remained unconvinced by these claims to the departed pastor's blessing, especially when Rutherford used a legal loophole to remove four opposing members of the board of directors (a majority) and replace them with his own partisans, in spite of the fact that Russell had appointed the four to serve on the board "for life" (*Faith on the March,* by A. H. Macmillan, p. 80). The removed directors served as the nucleus for opposition that eventually coalesced into Russellite organizations competing with the Watchtower Society.

In addition to such internal upheaval *The Finished Mystery* also brought down on Rutherford and his friends the wrath of the secular state. With the First World War raging, many were offended by a book that declared, "War is

in open and utter violation of Christianity" (p. 250) and
that prophesied this:

> God will pour out His wrath upon the worldly professing Chris-
> tians. . . . They shall be delivered into the hands of a revolted
> soldiery, brutal, destructive, pitiless, skilled in the arts of
> slaughter, taught by Teutons and Allies to know the utmost effi-
> ciency in war. (p. 469)

The book was banned in Canada, with possession of
a copy punishable by a fine of up to $5000 and imprison-
ment of up to five years. In the United States coauthor Clayton J. Woodworth was arrested, and "the United States
Department of Justice termed the distribution of *The Finished Mystery* a violation of the Espionage Act" (*1975 Yearbook of Jehovah's Witnesses,* p. 97). Eventually Woodworth,
Watchtower President J. F. Rutherford, and other men serv-
ing on the board of directors were sentenced to twenty years
each in the federal penitentiary, after a trial at which the
prosecution placed in evidence the preface plus pages
247–252, 406, 407, and 469 of *The Finished Mystery.* The
book's arguments against war were held to be part of a sedi-
tious conspiracy. When World War I ended, however, the
verdict was overturned by a higher court, the Watchtower
leaders were released after having spent nine months
behind bars, and the book continued to circulate. But the
existence today of many surviving copies with the offend-
ing pages cut out testifies to the furor this book once caused.

This seventh volume of Studies in the Scriptures is of
special interest to Watchtower watchers, not only for the
points already mentioned but also because it is an outstanding example of the organization's self-centered
approach to Scripture interpretation. A couple of examples are sufficient to demonstrate the tone of the entire book
in this regard. Note, first, how the commentary on Revelation 8:5 interprets this verse as prophetic of the Watchtower Society and its books:

> 8:5. *And the angel.*—THE WATCH TOWER SOCIETY through its
> proper representatives.
>   *Took the censer.*—The Seventh Volume of STUDIES IN THE
> SCRIPTURES, Divinely provided. . . .
>   *And there were [voices and] thunderings.*—Seven Volumes
> of "SCRIPTURE STUDIES," this one being the last of the series.
> (p. 145)

Equally self-centered and absurd to the objective observer is the application of Revelation 14:20, which identifies the winepress as "the Seventh Volume of *Scripture Studies,* the work that will squeeze the juice out of the 'Abominations of the earth'" (p. 229). The distance the blood flows out of the winepress is interpreted to mean the mileage from Scranton, Pennsylvania, where *The Finished Mystery* was written, to Brooklyn Bethel, where it was published—via "the Lackawanna Railroad . . . Hoboken Ferry . . . Barclay Street Ferry" and "Fulton Ferry" (p. 230).

Even the nonegocentric interpretations in *The Finished Mystery* tend to run contrary to current Watchtower teachings in ways that prove quite startling. For example, while the sect's leadership today interprets "Michael and his angels" at Revelation 12:7 to mean Jesus Christ (*alias* Michael the archangel) and subordinate angels, this book says that Michael is "the Pope" and his angels are "the Bishops" (p. 188). And in discussing Revelation 1:8 it says that "since His resurrection" Jesus can "be called the Almighty" (p. 15).

Also of interest is the fact that the great multitude of Revelation 7:9, which no man could number, is numbered here to "approximate 411,840,000" (p. 103).

While early editions identify "1917–1918" as the "one hour" spoken of in Revelation 18:17, ending in Babylon's destruction, later printings omit the dates (p. 285).

Although *The Finished Mystery* is no longer distributed by the Watchtower Society, it is still a potent weapon for creating controversy. Simply drop a copy into the hands of a thinking Jehovah's Witness, and see what happens. Few

JWs can read this volume without becoming quite upset over the teachings found in it. For that reason it has been removed from the libraries of most of their kingdom halls.

The Harp of God, by J. F. Rutherford, 1921

Early editions are subtitled *Proof Conclusive that Millions now Living will never Die,* with this further description on the title page: "A text-book for Bible study specially adapted for use of beginners; with numerous questions and Scripture citations."

In this his first hardcover book, Rutherford gives a simple presentation of essentially the same theology, chronology, and eschatology taught in Russell's Studies in the Scriptures. He uses a harp to represent the divine plan: "The ten strings of the harp, therefore, very fitly represent the ten great fundamental truths or doctrines of the divine plan" (p. 20), which correspond to the remaining ten chapter headings of his book: "Creation," "Justice Manifested," "The Abrahamic Promise," "The Birth of Jesus," "The Ransom," "Resurrection," "Mystery Revealed," "Our Lord's Return," "Glorification of the Church," and "Restoration."

This book contains perhaps two points of interest from an historical standpoint. The first is that changes in the 1928 edition reflect a major doctrinal shift of key importance. Prior to that time the reference to a "faithful and wise servant" at Matthew 24:45–47 had been interpreted as prophetic of C. T. Russell as God's special messenger to the church. Thus the pre-1928 editions of *The Harp of God* say:

> Without a doubt Pastor Russell filled the office for which the Lord provided and about which he spoke, and was therefore that wise and faithful servant, ministering to the household of faith meat in due season. (p. 239)

Since it was this supposed appointment from the Lord that gave Russell his great authority, rather than his being president of the Watchtower Society, the notion eventually posed problems for Rutherford, who succeeded to the presidency but not to the spiritual appointment. Portraying Rutherford as merely a clever lawyer who dishonestly seized control of the headquarters corporation, Russellite Bible Student splinter groups competed with him for the loyalty of congregations and individuals across the country. So, in 1928 Rutherford totally rewrote the section about Russell (pp. 235–241 in early editions; pp. 240–248 in the revised editions) to eliminate the thought of his being a special messenger. In fact, Russell's name does not even appear in the rewritten section.

This is important, because Jehovah's Witnesses today base their allegiance to the Watchtower Society on the belief that it is the mouthpiece or legal arm of God's faithful and discreet slave *class,* the remaining eight-thousand-odd members of the body of Christ said to be still alive on the earth. This was the new notion Rutherford introduced to replace the thought of Russell as "that servant" individually. Examination of the original teaching in *The Harp of God* can help a JW see that the Watchtower Society's claim to spiritual authority rests on a foundation of shifting sand.

The second point of interest is that *The Harp of God* speaks of "the year 1874, the date of our Lord's second presence" (p. 234, early editions; p. 240, later editions). This, of course, is to be expected in a book published in 1921, nine years before Rutherford moved the date of Christ's invisible return from 1874 to 1914, in the *Golden Age* magazine of 1930: "Jesus has been present since the year 1914" (p. 503). But the oddity is that, after introducing this important change, the Society produced new 1937 and 1940 editions of *The Harp of God* that retained the old 1874 date for Christ's presence.

All editions combined reached a total distribution of 5,819,037 copies in twenty-two languages, according to *Then Is Finished the Mystery of God* (p. 215).

The Way to Paradise, by W. E. Van Amburgh, 1924

The Watchtower Society's corporate secretary and treasurer from the days of Charles Taze Russell until 1947, the year of his own death, W. E. Van Amburgh wrote *The Way to Paradise* in "simple, pictorial language ... adapted to Intermediate Students of the Bible" according to the title page, or for "boys and girls" according to the introduction by J. F. Rutherford (p. iii).

Concerning "the great pyramid of Gizeh in Egypt" he reiterates and elaborates on Russell's earlier teachings:

> It is quite probable that Shem, the son of Noah, a faithful servant of God, was in charge of its construction. ... The pyramid also outlines in its own peculiar way the same plan of God that we find in the Bible, and it dated beforehand some of the most notable events that have occurred in the history of mankind. It gives the date of the exodus of the Children of Israel from Egypt, and the date of the birth and the death of Jesus. It gives the date of the French revolution as 1789, and the great World War as 1914, besides many more. (pp. 156–158)

Then he adds this:

> The Bible and "The Bible in Stone" give the date 1914 for the beginning of the great change. History proves that the ouster proceedings began promptly on time. Prophecy indicates that 1925–1926 will see the greater part of the ousting completed. (p. 171)

Continuing to prophesy concerning the years immediately following release of his book, Van Amburgh writes:

> When you take up a more advanced study of the Bible, you will find that the year 1925 A.D. is particularly marked in prophecy. (p. 220)
>
> We should, therefore, expect shortly after 1925 to see the awakening of Abel, Enoch, Noah, Abraham, Isaac, Jacob, Melchisedec, Job, Moses, Samuel, David, Isaiah, Jeremiah, Ezekiel, Daniel, John the Baptist, and others mentioned in the eleventh chapter of Hebrews. (p. 224)

These teachings all prove quite embarrassing to Jehovah's Witnesses today, and the book is not to be found on their kingdom hall library shelves. The organization's official *Watch Tower Publications Index 1930–1985* simply lists "1924, The Way to Paradise" with no references, indicating that the book is not mentioned in any other literature printed after 1929.

Kingdom Hymns, 1924–1926

Dated 1924 but not copyrighted until 1925 and not actually released until 1926, this small hardbound book of eighty songs with music was intended primarily for children in Watchtower families.

Comfort for the Jews, by J. F. Rutherford, 1925

A compilation and amplification of Rutherford's broadcast lectures on "Jews Returning to Palestine," this book claims that "it is the first unbiased presentation of the subject from the Scriptural viewpoint published" (p. 3). But a strongly Zionist tone is made clear in the publisher's foreword: "JUDGE RUTHERFORD, known through the world as a friend of the Hebrew people, is vigorously supporting the claim of the Jews to the Holy Land." In this, Rutherford was merely continuing the policies of his predecessor concerning whom a book has been published titled *Pastor Charles Taze Russell: An Early American Christian Zionist,* by David Horowitz (New York: Philosophical Library, 1986). Although today disavowing Zionism and holding a neutral position on Middle Eastern political and territorial issues, Jehovah's Witnesses still encounter hostility on the basis of their former stand.

The Watchtower Society has also reversed itself on the matter of converting Jews. Jehovah's Witnesses now actively seek to proselytize them, although the publisher's foreword in *Comfort for the Jews* says concerning J. F. Rutherford that "he is opposed to proselyting the Jews, holding that such is not only wrong but contrary to the Scriptures."

(*Note:* Much of the material found in *Comfort for the Jews* is reproduced word for word in Rutherford's later book *Life.*)

Deliverance, by J. F. Rutherford, 1926

Reminiscent of Mormonism, which presents Christ and the devil as brothers, the preface on page 5 says, "The names of the three great beings herein made conspicuous are: Jehovah the Father, and the Logos and Lucifer his sons." Another departure from orthodox theology, on page 12, is supported by quoting John 1:1–4 as saying:

> Originally was the Logos, and the Logos was with God; and the Logos was a God. The same was originally with God. All things through him came into existence; in him was life, and the life was the light of men.

The translation allegedly quoted is not identified, even though the "a God" rendering so casually presented here would not likely be found in any Bible that a reader might pick up off the shelf. *The Emphatic Diaglott* resorted to by Russell and Rutherford for other unusual renderings says that "a god was the Word" in its interlinear reading and "the LOGOS was God" in the main text—so Rutherford was not quoting from the *Emphatic Diaglott.* The Society's own *New World Translation* of John 1:1 ("the Word was a god") was not published until 1950, so obviously Rutherford was not quoting from it in 1926. Could it be then that no reference was made to any particular translation, in the hope that the reader would simply accept this wording as what "the Bible" says? In any case, failure to identify this variant rendering as such could not have been an oversight, since it is repeated through numerous editions and printings over a period of years.

Creation, by J. F. Rutherford, 1927

This book is subtitled or described on its title page thus:

> The Scriptural proof of the creation of things seen and unseen,
> showing the unfolding of the Divine Plan from the Logos to the
> completion of the royal family of heaven and the restoration
> of man.

It was published at the brink of an important transitional
period for the Watchtower organization. This is one of the
last books to promote the teaching that Christ returned
invisibly in the year 1874:

> The Scriptural proof is that the period of his presence and the
> day of God's preparation is a period from A.D. 1874 forward.
> The second coming of the Lord, therefore, began in 1874. (p.
> 310, early editions)

(In later editions the quotation is on page 289, and the date
reads "1874 A.D." instead of "A.D. 1874.") In 1930 Rutherford revised this chronology to say that "Jesus has been
present since the year 1914" (*Golden Age,* 1930, p. 503).
The change was introduced without explanation, apparently forced by the failure of a whole series of prophecies
based on the 1874 date. Supporting arguments for the
change from 1874 to 1914 were not presented until the book
The Truth Shall Make You Free was released in 1943 (see
discussion in our next chapter).

Jehovah's Witnesses today are shocked to discover that
several pages of *Creation* are devoted to the prophetic significance of the year 1799, offering "proof that 1799 definitely marks the beginning of 'the time of the end'" (p. 315,
early editions; p. 294, later editions). The sect nowadays
attaches no significance whatsoever to the year 1799.

Witnesses are also surprised to see the portrait of
Christ, his head adorned with a large halo, as a frontispiece
in early editions. This position opposite the title page is
left blank in later editions, but a halo still surrounds Christ's
head in the artwork titled "Resurrection," by Albert V.
Keller, found on page 208 in early editions and page 168
in later editions.

Also, at this time the Watchtower Society had not yet abandoned the use of the cross in favor of the upright pole its books show Jesus nailed to today. So, a traditional version of the crucifixion is illustrated on page 209 in early editions and page 265 in later editions, and the text states that Christ "died on the cross" (p. 192, early editions; p. 183, later editions).

Year Book, 1927

The first annual *Year Book,* in 1925, was actually a booklet featuring statistics on literature distribution, baptisms, and meeting attendance for the prior year, as well as personal testimonies and anecdotes from various lands. In 1927 it was upgraded to a book with the addition of daily Scripture readings and discussions to replace those found in *Daily Heavenly Manna for the Household of Faith* by Gertrude W. Seibert (1907). The change was because of J. F. Rutherford's view that the organization should no longer publish or distribute a book written by a woman.

The Watchtower Society continued to publish an annual *Yearbook of Jehovah's Witnesses* much like this one until 1986, when the daily Scripture texts were again separated into another volume.

Government, by J. F. Rutherford, 1928

With characteristic arrogance the author's foreword on page 5 announces that "what is set forth in the following pages is not the expressed opinion of man. The facts are plainly stated as they exist." Lumping together as the devil's organization virtually everything outside the Watchtower organization, the book's main point can be summarized by this statement on page 329: "The clergy, the profiteers and the politicians are in an alliance to govern the peoples of earth, and their god or invisible ruler is Satan the Devil, the prince of evil."

Noteworthy illustrations include, on page 66, a portrait of Christ with a large halo behind his head, a symbol Jehovah's Witnesses today reject as pagan; also a haunting picture of the devil on page 65 showing him as a naked olive-skinned man with piercing white eyes, and another on page 197 showing him seated on a dark cloud fingering a keyboard to manipulate a warring world below.

Reconciliation, by J. F. Rutherford, 1928

This volume presents Rutherford's interpretation of the fall of man and of God's actions to bring about man's reconciliation. He examines the Jewish law covenant and then the Christian new covenant. Perhaps because of the topics covered, this book seems milder in tone than many of Rutherford's other works. But his characteristic venom is manifested in the discussion of deity:

> Satan has used some of his agents, the clergy, to exalt the name of Jesus above that of Jehovah. . . . It is not a new trick of his. The Devil . . . has been teaching the doctrine of a trinity for a long while. . . . the clergy have gone on and still go on teaching the people the Satanic doctrines of the trinity and the incarnation. (pp. 136–137)

Also, reinforcing a teaching found earlier in *Thy Kingdom Come* by Charles T. Russell, *Reconciliation* again teaches that God resides on a star in the Pleiades constellation:

> The constellation of the seven stars forming the Pleiades. . . . It has been suggested, and with much weight, that one of the stars of that group is the dwelling-place of Jehovah. (p. 14)

Songs of Praise to Jehovah, 1928

Many of the 337 songs in this book were written by Watchtower adherents, but it also contains a number of older hymns borrowed and adapted from other churches.

Life, by J. F. Rutherford, 1929

This volume reproduces word for word much of the material from Rutherford's earlier book *Comfort for the Jews,* along with the addition of new chapters and illustrations. The chief of these is an eighty-seven-page commentary on Job that covers the Book of Job from beginning to end but skips several verses. This commentary presents Job's false comforters as picturing the Protestant and Catholic clergy, while Elihu pictures the Watchtower's followers.

Interestingly, the publisher's preface calls to mind the familiar line from Hamlet, "The lady doth protest too much," by asserting that

> THIS book is not propaganda. It is no part of a propaganda scheme. . . . The reader is not asked nor expected to join anything. He is not asked for nor expected to contribute money. . . .
> This is not a religious book. (p. 9)

Prophecy, by J. F. Rutherford, 1929

The Watchtower president here continues to maintain that "the Scriptural proof is that the second presence of the Lord Jesus Christ began in 1874 A.D." (p. 65). Moreover, just four years after the failure of his own prophecy that "1925 will mark the return of Abraham, Isaac, Jacob and the faithful prophets of old" (*Millions Now Living Will Never Die,* pp. 89–90), Rutherford here denounces "the clergymen or pastors of the various churches" as "false prophets" (p. 45).

Light (Book One), by J. F. Rutherford, 1930

This commentary covers Revelation, chapters 1 through 14, after dismissing all previous commentaries with the declaration that "prior to 1930 there never was a satisfactory explanation of the Revelation published" (pp. 5–6).

Have you ever wondered what time period is meant by the 1260 days mentioned at Revelation 12:6? You need look no farther than *Light (Book One)*. It says, "The period of 1260 days in the wilderness began March 27, 1919, and the end of that period came September 8, 1922" (p. 249). Why those dates? Rutherford explains:

> On March 26, 1919, the imprisoned officers of the Society were released, and immediately on the 27th day of March, 1919, efforts were begun to carry on the witness work. . . .
>
> The Lord caused his people to gather in convention in September, 1922, at Cedar Point, Ohio. . . . September 8 . . . the slogan was announced, "Advertise the King and the Kingdom"; and from that day forward the organized witness work began. That date was exactly the end of the 1260-day period. (pp. 249, 251)

The trumpet blasts from seven angels blowing trumpets in Revelation, chapters 8 and 9, are similarly interpreted as prophetic concerning the organization. They are said to symbolize resolutions passed annually at seven Watchtower conventions between the years 1922 and 1928.

Light (Book Two), by J. F. Rutherford, 1930

This commentary covers Revelation, chapters 15 through 22, plus portions of Daniel, chapter 2.

It identifies the pouring out of the seven bowls of God's wrath in Revelation, chapter 16, as prophetic of resolutions passed at Watchtower conventions between 1922 and 1928—the same resolutions that were allegedly prophesied by the seven angelic trumpet blasts of Revelation, chapters 8 and 9.

But Rutherford does not apply *all* of Revelation in this egocentric manner to the Watchtower organization. He minces no words in applying Revelation 17:1 to the other churches:

> "The great whore" is the Devil's religion, mislabeled "organized Christianity" or "Christendom", and which forms a part of Satan's organization. (p. 81)

Vindication (Book One), by J. F. Rutherford, 1931

This commentary discusses the Book of Ezekiel, chapters 1 through 24, taking virtually every verse as prophetic of the Watchtower Society and its circumstances from 1914 onward. Because it foretold these "recent events," says Rutherford, "this shows why the prophecy of Ezekiel could not be understood prior to 1918" (p. 17).

An unusual admission of prophetic failure is found on page 146:

> God's faithful people on the earth emphasized the importance of the dates 1914 and 1918 and 1925. They had much to say about these dates and what would come to pass, but all they predicted did not come to pass.

Although he goes on to make excuses and to defend the Watchtower Society, the admission that its prophecies did not come to pass is devastating, because it puts the organization in the category of false prophets condemned by God in Deuteronomy, chapter 18:

> However, the prophet who presumes to speak in my name a word that I have not commanded him to speak . . . that prophet must die. . . . when the prophet speaks in the name of Jehovah and the word does not occur or come true. (vv. 20–22, New World Translation)

Still, with a few words Rutherford smooths over the fact that Watchtower prophecies for 1914, 1918, and 1925 proved false. Then in the next breath he goes on to discuss Ezekiel, chapter 13, identifying "those who prophesy falsely" as "the clergy" and other opposers of the Watchtower message (pp. 148, 150).

The words at Ezekiel 13:17 about "the daughters of thy people" are interpreted as prophetic of the role of women in Christendom during the early twentieth century. The fact that "in 1919 . . . the Congress of the United States enfranchised women" is seen as part of Satan's preparation of "his forces for Armageddon" (p. 155). And the fact that "'Mother's Day' was observed in America first in 1914" is presented as part of a satanic plot:

On the face of it the arrangement of "Mother's Day" seems harm-
less and calculated to do good. But the people are in ignorance
of Satan's subtle hand in the matter, and that he is back of the
movement, to turn the people away from God. (pp. 158–159)

When assessing the Watchtower Society's view of
women as presented in *Vindication* and elsewhere, it
should be kept in mind that the organization was ruled for
more than a hundred years by men who had problems with
the opposite sex. Both Russell[1] and Rutherford lived apart
from estranged wives; Knorr did not marry until he was
around forty years old; and Franz lived as a bachelor all
his life.

Preservation, by J. F. Rutherford, 1932

This commentary on the books of Esther and Ruth
interprets both as prophetic of events relating to the Watchtower organization from 1914 onward. For example, it
states that "Ruth particularly pictures that class of God's
children who were brought into the temple, and hence into
God's organization, from and after 1922" (p. 255). Rutherford admits that "*The Watchtower* of November 15, 1902,
said this: '. . . the book of Ruth is not prophetical, but merely
historical'" (p. 174). But later he explains that the alleged
prophetic fulfillments in the 1920s "clearly show why that
book could not be understood in earlier days" (p. 255).

Vindication (Book Two), by J. F. Rutherford, 1932

This commentary continues the discussion of the
Book of Ezekiel, covering chapters 25 through 39.

Readers who expect a real Bible commentary may be
surprised to find a ten-page section (pp. 168–179) devoted
to the National Banking Act of the United States and com-
posed primarily of correspondence between "Rothschild
Brothers, bankers of London, and Ikleheimer, Morton and
Vandergould, of Wall Street, New York" (p. 171). But this

is included because the book consists mainly of an attack on "Big Business."

Although many abuses of commercial power are justifiably condemned, there seems to be one perceived offense against the Watchtower itself that may have been the underlying cause of the organization's big guns being turned against big business:

> Big Business . . . controls all the choice radio frequencies or channels and refuses to use any of these, or to permit their facilities to be used, for broadcasting the message of God's kingdom. (p. 64)

> The clergy, the false prophets of Satan's organization, and who are hirelings of Big Business . . . deny to Jehovah's servants the use of the facilities now controlled by Big Business and which might be used to spread the message of the Lord's kingdom. (p. 184)

The Watchtower Society's use of radio was at its peak at this time, employing the facilities of between three hundred and four hundred radio stations to broadcast Rutherford's speeches. The history in *Jehovah's Witnesses in the Divine Purpose* refers to the struggle to maintain this radio network as "The Battle of the Air Waves" (pp. 122, 134). Rutherford turned his commentary on Ezekiel into one of the battlefields.

Vindication (Book Three), by J. F. Rutherford, 1932

This commentary concludes the discussion of the Book of Ezekiel, covering chapters 40 through 48. It also discusses Haggai and the third chapter of Zechariah. But before the verse-by-verse consideration begins, the first hundred pages of the book feature a topical discussion taken mainly from Second Kings, chapters 9 and 10, that focuses on the personalities involved—Jehu, Jehonadab, Elisha, Ahab, Jezebel—each of whom is interpreted as prophetic of some aspect of the Watchtower Society's circumstances.

But perhaps the most significant statement in *Vindication (Book Three)* is found in the advertisement at the back of the book for thirteen of J. F. Rutherford's booklets. It says:

> Each treatise can be read in just fifteen minutes, and more genuine satisfaction and profitable pleasure derived therefrom in that length of time than can be gotten from studying the Bible by yourself in a whole year. (p. 383)

So, spending fifteen minutes with Rutherford's writings is considered more valuable than a year with the Bible.

Preparation, by J. F. Rutherford, 1933

This book is a commentary on the entire Book of Zechariah. It interprets virtually everything the prophet wrote as foretelling events that surrounded the Watchtower organization from 1914 through the early 1930s.

Consider, for example, the application of Zechariah 14:14, which speaks of Judah fighting at Jerusalem and the wealth of the pagan nations being gathered together. Rutherford uses this verse to lash out at those he perceives as the Watchtower Society's enemies:

> This prophecy shows that the nations, and particularly "Christendom", bring all of their wealth and power against Jehovah's organization. . . . Big Business, acting by its hirelings, now grabs the radio stations and other means of communication between the people, and uses such for its own selfish purposes and against Jehovah. . . . He now has these pig-headed, big-headed "roosters" on earth in complete derision, and laughs at them when they boast about what they are doing in preventing his message from being heard. (pp. 320–321)

This is the same complaint Rutherford airs in commenting on Ezekiel in *Vindication (Book Two)* published the previous year, namely that he was encountering difficulty in securing radio time to broadcast his lectures. He looks forward to broadcasting in the coming kingdom when "everybody on earth" will listen to only "one grand radio station operating without interference, and with unlimited power" (p. 332).

While most of the Book of Zechariah is applied to the Watchtower's struggles against "the commercial, political and religious element of Satan's organization" (p. 343), Rutherford also takes opportunities throughout the book to inveigh against his enemies within the sect, "the 'elective elders' who have assumed to be overseers of the flock of God, but who fail and refuse to obey God's commandments and to feed upon up-to-date truth which Jehovah has provided for his own" (p. 199). These are locally elected elders Rutherford removed in his campaign to tighten central control over the congregations of his followers; though removed from official positions of power, many of them remained members of their local congregations. Rutherford complains that they "murmur, find fault with the work, weep and wail because they do not have their own way and because they are not permitted further to serve as 'elective elders'" (p. 359). Such attacks in the Society's literature made it uncomfortable for such men to remain even as members of the organization, because the attacks were viewed as coming not from Rutherford personally but from God:

> As surely as Jehovah has an organization on the earth, just so surely he is feeding the members of that organization by the hand of Christ Jesus. The facts prove that he uses the Watch Tower publications to bring these truths to the attention of his remnant. (p. 176)

Jehovah, by J. F. Rutherford, 1934

The first hundred pages of this book discuss Moses and the ten plagues upon Egypt, showing each of the plagues to have been prophetic of some proclamation or action by the Watchtower organization during the post-World War I period. Summarizing this portion Rutherford writes:

> The people are here warned of a wicked conspiracy formed by Satan, and in which conspiracy there are joined the inter-

national bankers, the unfaithful clergy, and the conscienceless
politicians, among the purposes of which conspiracy are these:
To put America into the League of Nations, control the money
and all other property, rule the people by the hand of their one-
man dictator, destroy the freedom of speech and press, and stop
the true worship of God and Christ. (p. 24)

The remainder of the book examines the various
covenants found in the Old and New Testaments, again
making application to the sect and its followers. Consider,
for example, "'the covenant, which the Lord commanded
Moses to make with the children of Israel in the land of
Moab . . .'—Deut. 29:1" (p. 262). Rutherford asserts that
"the covenant here in Moab specifically refers to the remnant. The building up of Zion took place in 1918. . . . The
facts show that these prophecies began to have fulfillment
in the year 1918" (pp. 273–274).

The teaching on the "great multitude" of Revelation 7:9
found on page 159 is significant, because Rutherford reversed
it in a speech to a Witness convention the following year. In
1935 he introduced the belief that JWs hold today, namely
that the "great multitude" pictures faithful Witnesses who
will live forever on earth and not go to heaven with the elite
group of 144,000 alleged to make up the body of Christ. Thus
the vast majority of the 10 million now attending kingdom
halls see themselves as part of this "great crowd" or "great
multitude." But here in the book *Jehovah* Rutherford teaches
that the great multitude of Revelation 7:9 designates God-
fearing people who "remain in the selfish organizations
called 'church denominations', being induced to do so by
fear, coercion and influence wrongfully exercised by the
clergy of those denominations" (p. 159).

Elsewhere, Rutherford stresses to his followers "the
necessity of being entirely obedient to the instructions coming to them through God's organization" (p. 299).

This book also repudiates the Society's earlier teaching that the departed spirit of Pastor Russell was still direct-

ing the organization from beyond the grave (see the discussion of *The Finished Mystery,* 1917). Rutherford now writes:

> No one of the temple company will be so foolish as to conclude that some brother (or brethren) at one time amongst them, and who has died and gone to heaven, is now instructing the saints on earth and directing them as to their work. (p. 191)

Riches, by J. F. Rutherford, 1936

Organized by topic, this book covers a number of areas, but by far the most attention is given to the Roman Catholic hierarchy, the subject of a seventy-page chapter titled "Philistines." Why such a title? Because Rutherford freely adds prophetic significance to early features of Israel's history and asserts that "the Philistines pictured or foreshadowed the Roman Catholic Hierarchy" (p. 227).

Perhaps even more boldly the Watchtower Society's second president dismisses all Protestant churches (including Evangelicals) with the stroke of a pen:

> The Roman Catholic Hierarchy is the official government that controls and rules the religion of so-called "Christendom". What was at one time known as "Protestantism" is now dead, and the so-called "Protestants" are dominated and controlled by the Roman Catholic Hierarchy. Protestantism exists only in name, not in fact. (p. 228)

While most knowledgeable individuals would view such an assertion as not worth the dignity of a rebuttal, Rutherford's followers accepted his word as gospel.

JW attacks on Catholicism make interesting reading, because they usually furnish numerous instances of "the pot calling the kettle black." Rutherford's book *Riches* is no exception. Consider, for example, this accusation:

> If anyone dared to express his opinion contrary to the doctrines taught by the clergy of the Roman Catholic organization, that one was straightway charged with heresy. (p. 246)

Jehovah's Witnesses know that if anyone dares to express his opinion contrary to the doctrines taught by the leaders of the Watchtower organization, that one is straightway charged with apostasy. The only difference is that the Catholic Church formerly exercised sufficient secular influence to have its heretics silenced through corporal punishment, while, lacking the power to inflict bodily harm, the Watchtower silences its apostates by enforced shunning, cutting them off from family and friends inside the sect. But the attitude toward free thought among Jehovah's Witnesses is much the same as it was among Catholics under the Inquisition. And, while a Witness accused of apostasy need not fear for his life as did a Catholic accused of heresy during the Inquisition, the Witness may face the loss of housing and employment, if these are provided by fellow JWs, and he will be told that he eventually will face death at the hands of angelic executioners.

After attacking the Catholic hierarchy's claim to authority, Rutherford goes on to present his own organization as the one God has placed in charge:

> Jehovah has made the necessary arrangements within his organization to instruct his people, and all recognize that for some years *The Watchtower* has been the means of communicating information to God's people. That does not mean that those who prepare the manuscript for *The Watchtower* are inspired, but rather it means that the Lord through his angels sees to it that the information is given to his people in due time. (p. 316)

With good reason one might wonder whether Rutherford was truly opposed on principle to papal rule. It may have been simply a case of rivalry, the pope seated at Rome arousing jealousy in the one seated at Brooklyn.

Enemies, by J. F. Rutherford, 1937
This book, even more so than *Riches,* singles out the Roman Catholic Church for attack. On page 286 Ruther-

ford ties together his arguments concerning "enemies" in this brief summary:

> From all the evidence the conclusion is irresistible that the Roman Catholic Hierarchy organization serves the Devil and is therefore the enemy of God, the enemy of man, and the very personification of unrighteousness.

But Rutherford does not stop with an indictment of the Roman Catholic religion. He goes on to warn of a dark plot to take over America. The first hint of this is found in the middle of the book, where he cautions that "the United States government has a Roman Catholic as postmaster general . . . who is in fact an agent and representative of the Vatican" (p. 178). Later, besides claiming that the visit of a Vatican official to this country helped bring about the re-election of Franklin Delano Roosevelt in 1936, he asserts that "it is well known, by every person in America who really thinks, that the determination of the Roman Catholic Hierarchy is to gain control of the United States and make it a government similar to that of Germany and Italy," then ruled by Hitler's Nazis and Mussolini's Fascists (p. 291). Will this foul ambition succeed? Two years before the outbreak of World War II in Europe, the Watchtower's president prophesies as follows:

> The question is, Will Great Britain and America become Fascist under the dominating control of the Roman Catholic Hierarchy? The Scriptures and the facts appear to fully support that conclusion. (p. 291)

Then he goes on to discuss "the prophecy of the Lord" about the time "when the Hierarchy has gained complete temporal power of the earth" and "the League of Nations" will become "in fact a league of Fascism or combined Fascist governments, dominated by the Roman Catholic Hierarchy" (p. 292). This prophecy published by the Watchtower Society in 1937 is often overlooked when commentators enumerate the sect's better-known prophetic failures concerning the years 1914, 1925, and 1975.

Salvation, by J. F. Rutherford, 1939

The title page identifies this as "a text book for the Jonadabs." This name *Jonadabs* is applied to a secondary class of believers, outside the body of Christ, who receive "blessings from the Lord on the earth" instead of going to heaven (p. 66). Rutherford first introduced this teaching in 1935, declaring the "great multitude" or "great crowd" of Revelation 7:9 to be such a class. The man Jonadab, son of Rechab, who joined Jehu on his chariot, and the Rechabite people who lived among the Israelites as servants, are selected by Rutherford to illustrate this secondary class of believers (2 Kings 10:15, 16; Jer. 35:18, 19). The illustration is still employed occasionally today, but the term *Jonadabs* is no longer used on an everyday basis to describe the "other sheep" with an earthly hope.

In this book Rutherford also uses the term *Jehovah's Witnesses* in a limited sense to refer not to all of his followers but only to "the little flock or remnant,"—the remaining ones of the 144,000 who, he taught, were destined for heaven (p. 142). Today the Watchtower Society includes under the name Jehovah's Witnesses all of the baptized individuals who offer the organization's literature in house-to-house ministry. These now number somewhat over 4 million, of whom around eight thousand are said to be of the "little flock" going to heaven; the rest have been taught to expect an earthly reward. Of the more than 10 million regularly attending JW kingdom halls, the remaining 6 million are new converts, children too young to report door-to-door activity, and inactive backslidden adults, none of whom are counted as Witnesses.

As "a text book for the Jonadabs," then, *Salvation* is a tool for teaching new followers Rutherford's version of the plan of salvation. Since he asserts that the door to heaven has already been closed, converts are instructed in the earthly hope. Thus, chapter 3, titled "Great Multitude" and devoted to presenting that secondary hope, covers 106 pages or nearly a third of the book.

But perhaps the most interesting page is 311, which carries the heading "Beth-Sarim" and begins, "At San Diego, California, there is a small piece of land, on which, in the year 1929, there was built a house, which is called and known as Beth-Sarim. The Hebrew words *Beth Sarim* mean 'House of Princes.'" On the following page is an artist's sketch of the mansion. It was to be occupied by several Old Testament characters who were expected to be resurrected prior to Armageddon to serve as princes over the earth. However, the expectation went unfulfilled, and Rutherford died in the house in January 1942. It was later sold quietly.

Religion, by J. F. Rutherford, 1940

"Religion Is a Snare and a Racket" (p. 383). That slogan emblazoned placards carried by groups of Jehovah's Witnesses in 1938 and 1939 as they staged "information marches" down city streets past Catholic and Protestant churches. The Watchtower Society's president uses the term *religion* similarly in this book to mean all forms of worship other than his own. In fact, Jehovah's Witnesses continued to employ their own private definition of the word until "*The Watchtower* of March 15, 1951, approved of using the adjectives 'true' and 'false' respecting religion" (*1975 Yearbook of Jehovah's Witnesses,* p. 225).

The book *Religion* declares that "organized religion is the enemy of God, and the destructive foe of the people" (p. 162). Introductory chapters argue that the Catholic, Protestant, and Jewish clergy are joined together with political and financial leaders in a worldwide conspiracy against God. In building his case Rutherford points to "President Roosevelt's letter to the pope, and his appointment of an ambassador to the Vatican" and makes allegations that "the Roman

Catholic Hierarchy has placed some trusted representative in every organization of the metropolitan press" (pp. 97, 94).

The final two-thirds of the book consists of a verse-by-verse commentary on the Book of Joel, in which the entire prophecy is interpreted as applying to the world scene during Rutherford's presidency of the Watchtower organization. The locusts that Joel sees sweeping over the land like an army are Jehovah's Witnesses spreading their message from house to house. The ancient city Tyre named in Joel's prophecy symbolizes "the Roman Catholic Hierarchy organization," and Sidon pictures "the heathen religions which are much older and from which the Papacy sprang," both of which persecute Rutherford's followers (pp. 303–304). The plundering of Tyre and Sidon he interprets as prophetically meaning that the Nazis and Fascists will plunder the Vatican:

> It is said that Vatican City has stored up more gold and other riches than any other nation or organization. It may be expected that the various deluded radical elements will swoop down on the Vatican and Hierarchy after they have finished the Jews. (p. 315)

However, the war in Europe did not proceed as Rutherford expected, and his prophecy proved false.

Children, by J. F. Rutherford, 1941

Set in large type and phrased in simple language, *Children* is intended to be read by children. Much of it consists of dialogue between fictitious characters, eighteen-year-old Eunice Rogers and twenty-year-old John Alden, who have both finished school and are planning to be married. But, in the course of studying the Bible together they learn that it advises against marriage and childbearing at this critical time so close to Armageddon:

> Should men and women, both of whom are Jonadabs or "other sheep" of the Lord, now marry before Armageddon and bring

forth children? They may choose to do so, but the admonition
or advice of the Scriptures appears to be against it. (p. 312)

So, John and Eunice decide to put off marriage until after
Armageddon, meanwhile living apart in their parents'
homes and devoting all of their time and energy to carrying the Watchtower's message from house to house. The
book ends on that note, as young John and Eunice join
hands and lift their voices in a song of praise.

J. F. Rutherford died more than fifty years ago, a few
months after the release of his book *Children*. He had written in it that "Armageddon is very near" (p. 151). But, if
John and Eunice were real people and postponing marriage
until after Armageddon, they would now both be in their
seventies. And the sad fact is that the millions of *Children*
books distributed actually did lead many young Johns and
Eunices to postpone marriage in the expectation that
Armageddon was "very near." Some of them have since
died old, alone, and bitter.

Booklets

Watchtower booklets, almost too numerous to mention,
are simply listed here. Only those of lasting significance are
discussed. Most of those listed below are printed transcripts
of talks given by J. F. Rutherford over the radio or at major
conventions. An advertisement for thirteen of Rutherford's
booklets in *Vindication (Book Three)* states that "each trea-
tise can be read in just fifteen minutes, and more genuine
satisfaction and profitable pleasure derived therefrom in
that length of time than can be gotten from studying the Bible
by yourself in a whole year" (p. 383). Such a boast notwith-
standing, the Bible itself continues to be read, whereas these
booklets now sit on shelves as collector's items.

A Great Battle in the Ecclesiastical Heavens, by Joseph
F. Rutherford, 1915

Although written by Rutherford, this booklet was published during Russell's presidency and is therefore discussed in our previous chapter.

Berean Studies on The Finished Mystery, 1917

Harvest Siftings (Parts I and II), 1917

This brochure or booklet was produced by J. F. Rutherford during the period of factional infighting following Russell's death. Opposed by a majority of the Society's board of directors, Rutherford spared no weapon in his struggle for control of the organization. As a lawyer he skillfully unseated the directors Russell had appointed for life, and as a communicator he destroyed them in the eyes of his readers.

Open warfare was triggered in the sect's Brooklyn offices when Rutherford released *The Finished Mystery,* volume 7 of Studies in the Scriptures. (He had prepared the publication without the consent or even the knowledge of the hostile directors.) Most of the issues in the internal struggle revolved around personalities and therefore are of little interest today except insofar as they demonstrate the human rather than divine nature of the Watchtower organization. *Harvest Siftings* presents only Rutherford's side of the dispute, of course. His opponents published a twenty-four-page refutation under the title *Light after Darkness,* which is still circulated by present-day Russellite groups.

Rutherford's *Harvest Siftings* booklet is not to be confused with the *Zion's Watch Tower and Herald of Christ's Presence (Extra Edition)—A Conspiracy Exposed: Harvest Siftings,* produced by Charles T. Russell in 1894.

The Revelation of Jesus Christ, 1918

Berean Studies on Tabernacle Shadows of the "Better Sacrifices," 1918

Can the Living Talk With the Dead? (Talking With the Dead?), by J. F. Rutherford, 1920

Millions Now Living Will Never Die, by J. F. Rutherford, 1920

Today we would call this booklet of 126 pages a paper-back book. It was released in the midst of a 1918–1922 campaign featuring a public lecture that was originally titled, "The World Has Ended—Millions Now Living Will Never Die."[2] (Some recent Watchtower publications[3] apparently try to save face by referring to the lecture as "Millions Now Living May Never Die," and the talk may indeed have been advertised that way in certain cities, but the booklet carries the more positively stated title, ". . . *Will* Never Die.")

Jehovah's Witnesses may argue that millions who were alive when this booklet went to press in 1920 are in fact still alive today (1993), namely, everyone who is over seventy-three years old. So, the possibility is still open that millions of them will never die. But that is not what Rutherford meant by the slogan. He meant that millions of his followers would gain everlasting life in 1925, just five years from his time of writing the words *now living* in 1920. He clarifies this thought on page 97:

> 1925 shall mark the resurrection of the faithful worthies of old and the beginning of reconstruction . . . millions of people now on the earth will be still on the earth in 1925. Then, based upon the promises set forth in the divine Word, we must reach the positive and indisputable conclusion that millions now living will never die. (p. 97)

According to this publication, "the old world legally ended in 1914 and the process of removing the worn out systems is now progressing, preparatory to the inauguration of Messiah's kingdom" (p. 19). In 1925 the kingdom would grant everlasting life to millions and would also resurrect "the faithful worthies of old" (p. 97). This would not be a spiritual event, like the purported invisible return of Christ, discernible only by the elect, but would be a physical resurrection to human life on earth:

> Scriptures definitely fix the fact that there will be a resurrec-
> tion of Abraham, Isaac, Jacob and other faithful ones of old . . .
> we may expect 1925 to witness the return of these faithful men
> of Israel from the condition of death, being resurrected and
> fully restored to perfect humanity and made the visible, legal
> representatives of the new order of things on earth. (p. 88)
>
> Therefore we may confidently expect that 1925 will mark
> the return of Abraham, Isaac, Jacob and the faithful prophets of
> old, particularly those named by the Apostle in Hebrews chap-
> ter eleven, to the condition of human perfection. (pp. 89–90)

When 1925 came and went with no earthly resurrection, Rutherford was forced to admit he had been wrong.
Governing Body member Karl Klein recalled about Rutherford, "Regarding his misguided statements as to what we
could expect in 1925, he once confessed to us at Bethel, 'I
made an ass of myself'" (*The Watchtower,* October 1, 1984,
p. 24). God, speaking at Deuteronomy 18:20–22, views the
matter more seriously and prescribes the death penalty for
a man whose failed predictions prove him to be a false
prophet. Clearly, the statements quoted here from *Millions
Now Living Will Never Die* prove quite embarrassing to the
Watchtower Society today.

The Bible on Our Lord's Return, by J. F. Rutherford, 1922

World Distress—Why? The Remedy, by J. F. Rutherford, 1923

A Desirable Government, by J. F. Rutherford, 1924

Hell, by J. F. Rutherford, 1924

Comfort for the People, by J. F. Rutherford, 1925

Our Lord's Return, by J. F. Rutherford, 1925

Year Book, 1925

This contained the year's report on literature distribution and meeting attendance. In 1927 the annual *Year Book*
was upgraded from a booklet to a book, with the addition
of daily Scripture readings to replace those found in *Daily*

Heavenly Manna for the Household of Faith by Gertrude W. Seibert (1907).

The Standard for the People, by J. F. Rutherford, 1926

Freedom for the Peoples, by J. F. Rutherford, 1927

Questions on Deliverance, by J. F. Rutherford, 1927

Restoration, by J. F. Rutherford, 1927

Where Are the Dead? by J. F. Rutherford, 1927

Prosperity Sure, by J. F. Rutherford, 1928

The Last Days, by J. F. Rutherford, 1928

The Peoples Friend, by J. F. Rutherford, 1928

Judgment, by J. F. Rutherford, 1929

Oppression, When Will It End? by J. F. Rutherford, 1929

Crimes and Calamities. The Cause. The Remedy, by J. F. Rutherford, 1930

Prohibition and the League of Nations, by J. F. Rutherford, 1930

In 1929 Congress strengthened Prohibition in the United States by enacting the Jones Law, which provided heavy fines and prison sentences for persons convicted of selling, manufacturing, transporting, exporting, or importing liquor. The following year Rutherford attacked Prohibition in a radio broadcast that was then published in booklet form. Canadian historian M. James Penton reports in his book *Apocalypse Delayed: The Story of Jehovah's Witnesses*[4] that "high Watch Tower officials at Brooklyn" who were fond of alcohol engaged in rum-running, having officials at the Canadian branch headquarters in Toronto smuggle liquor across the border into New York.

War or Peace, Which? by J. F. Rutherford, 1930

Heaven and Purgatory, by J. F. Rutherford, 1931

The Kingdom, the Hope of the World, by J. F. Rutherford, 1931

This sixty-four-page booklet contains the resolution voted at the Columbus, Ohio, Watchtower convention on July 26, 1931, which adopted the name Jehovah's Witnesses. Perhaps the most enlightening portion of the resolution is this, which explains why a new name was needed:

> WHEREAS shortly following the death of Charles T. Russell a division arose between those associated with him in such work, resulting in a number of such withdrawing from the Watch Tower Bible & Tract Society, and who have since refused to cooperate with said Society and its work and who decline to concur in the truth as published by the Watch Tower Bible & Tract Society, in *The Watch Tower* and the other recent publications of the above-named corporations, and have opposed and do now oppose the work of said Society in declaring the present message of God's kingdom and the day of the vengeance of our God against all parts of Satan's organization; and said opposing ones have formed themselves into divers and numerous companies and have taken and now bear such names as, to wit, "Bible Students," "Associated Bible Students," "Russellites teaching the truth as expounded by Pastor Russell," "Stand-Fasters," and like names, all of which tends to cause confusion and misunderstanding. (pp. 30–31)

So, the selection of a new name was necessitated by the split in the organization some fifteen years earlier. While Rutherford and his followers kept control over the legal corporations and therefore over the name "Watch Tower," those who refused to follow Rutherford were able to continue calling themselves "Bible Students" or "Russellites." When it became clear that these groups would not quickly die out or fade away, Rutherford selected a new denominational name for his followers. This move repudiated the position Russell had set forth in the early days of the sect:

> We believe that a visible organization, and the adoption of some particular name, would tend to increase our numbers and make us more respectable in the estimation of the world. . . . But . . . we always refuse to be called by any other name than that of our Head—Christians. (*Zion's Watch Tower,* March, 1883, p. 458, reprints)

Cause of Death, by J. F. Rutherford, 1932

Good News, by J. F. Rutherford, 1932

Health and Life, by J. F. Rutherford, 1932

Hereafter, by J. F. Rutherford, 1932

Home and Happiness, by J. F. Rutherford, 1932

Keys of Heaven, by J. F. Rutherford, 1932

Liberty, by J. F. Rutherford, 1932

The Final War, by J. F. Rutherford, 1932

What Is Truth? by J. F. Rutherford, 1932

What You Need, by J. F. Rutherford, 1932

Where Are the Dead? by J. F. Rutherford, 1932

Who Is God? by J. F. Rutherford, 1932

Dividing the People, by J. F. Rutherford, 1933

Escape to the Kingdom, by J. F. Rutherford, 1933

Intolerance, by J. F. Rutherford, 1933

The Crisis, by J. F. Rutherford, 1933

Angels, by J. F. Rutherford, 1934
    This sixty-four-page booklet outlines J. F. Rutherford's view of angels and demons. The brightly illustrated cover depicts an angelic being radiating his influence on distributors of Watchtower literature, while a demonic being exercises his invisible control over the clergy and the wealthy class.

Beyond the Grave, by J. F. Rutherford, 1934

Favored People, by J. F. Rutherford, 1934

His Vengeance, by J. F. Rutherford, 1934

His Works, by J. F. Rutherford, 1934

Righteous Ruler, by J. F. Rutherford, 1934

Supremacy, by J. F. Rutherford, 1934

Truth—Shall It Be Suppressed? by J. F. Rutherford, 1934

Why Pray for Prosperity? by J. F. Rutherford, 1934

World Recovery, by J. F. Rutherford, 1934

Government—Hiding the Truth. Why? by J. F. Rutherford, 1935

Loyalty, by J. F. Rutherford, 1935

Universal War Near, by J. F. Rutherford, 1935

Who Shall Rule the World? by J. F. Rutherford, 1935

Choosing. Riches or Ruin? by J. F. Rutherford, 1936

Protection, by J. F. Rutherford, 1936

Armageddon, by J. F. Rutherford, 1937

Model Study No. 1, by J. F. Rutherford, 1937

Safety, by J. F. Rutherford, 1937

Uncovered, by J. F. Rutherford, 1937

Cure, by J. F. Rutherford, 1938
     In his 1940 book *Religion* Rutherford boasts that the booklet *Cure,* "which contains a succinct statement of the falsity of religion and what is Christianity," had already achieved a circulation of more than 12 million (*Religion,* p. 158).

Face the Facts, by J. F. Rutherford, 1938
     This sixty-four-page booklet is composed of the text of two speeches delivered by J. F. Rutherford: "Face the Facts" and "Fill the Earth."

"Face the Facts" created considerable controversy by asserting that "the Roman Catholic Hierarchy of Authority, the Fascists and the Nazis are conspiring together to gain control and rule all the nations by dictators. . . . Religion is therefore a snare and a racket" (pp. 30–31).

"Fill the Earth" had a far-reaching effect on the lives of Rutherford's followers and future generations of Jehovah's Witnesses by telling them that it would be wrong for them to marry and have children:

> Would it be Scripturally proper for them to now marry and to begin to rear children? No, is the answer, which is supported by the Scriptures. . . . The Scriptures fully support the conclusion that the filling of the earth is not due to begin before, but after Armageddon. (pp. 46–47)

Many Jehovah's Witnesses have remained single or childless in obedience to this teaching, some deeply regretting it later in life.

Warning, by J. F. Rutherford, 1938

Advice for Kingdom Publishers, by J. F. Rutherford, 1939

Government and Peace, by J. F. Rutherford, 1939

Liberty to Preach, by J. F. Rutherford, 1939

Model Study No. 2, by J. F. Rutherford, 1939

Neutrality, by J. F. Rutherford, 1939

Order of Trial, 1939

Conspiracy Against Democracy, by J. F. Rutherford, 1940

End of Nazism, by J. F. Rutherford, 1940

Judge Rutherford Uncovers Fifth Column, by J. F. Rutherford, 1940

Refugees, by J. F. Rutherford, 1940

Satisfied, by J. F. Rutherford, 1940

Comfort All That Mourn, by J. F. Rutherford, 1941

This is the text of a talk by the same title delivered by Rutherford on August 10, 1941, at a Watchtower convention in St. Louis, Missouri, his home state. It interprets Daniel, chapter 11, as predicting the end of the Axis powers of World War II. On the day the talk was given, 450,000 copies of the booklet were distributed to conventioneers, who in turn passed them on to the public.

God and the State, by J. F. Rutherford, 1941

Jehovah's Servants Defended, by J. F. Rutherford, 1941

Model Study No. 3, by J. F. Rutherford, 1941

Theocracy, by J. F. Rutherford, 1941

Tracts and Pamphlets

Rutherford-era tracts and pamphlets are almost too numerous to mention. They are simply listed here.

The Bible Students Monthly (The Fall of Babylon), 1917

Kingdom News No. 1 (Religious Intolerance—Pastor Russell's Followers Persecuted Because They Tell the People the Truth—Treatment of Bible Students Smacks of the "Dark Ages," 1918

Kingdom News No. 2 ("The Finished Mystery" and Why Suppressed—Clergymen Take a Hand), 1918

Kingdom News No. 3 (Two Great Battles Raging—Fall of Autocracy Certain—Satanic Strategy Doomed to Failure—The Birth of Antichrist), 1918

Calamities—Why Permitted? 1918

Christian Science, 1918

Comforting Words of Life, 1918

Demons Infest Earth's Atmosphere, 1918

Do You Believe in the Resurrection? 1918

Do You Know? 1918

Earth to Be Filled With Glory, 1918

Gathering the Lord's Jewels, 1918

Golden Age at the Door, 1918

Hope of Immortality, 1918

Is There a God? 1918

Is the Soul Immortal? 1918

Joyful Message for the Sin-Sick, 1918

Our Responsibility as Christians, 1918

Predestination and Election, 1918

Spiritism Is Demonism, 1918

The Bruising of Satan, 1918

The Case of the International Bible Students Association, 1918

The Dawn of a New Era, 1918

The Liberty of the Gospel, 1918

The Rich Man in Hell, 1918

Thieves in Paradise, 1918

Weeping All Night, 1918

What Is the Soul? 1918

Where Are the Dead? 1918

Why God Permits Evil, 1918

Proclamation—A Challenge to World Leaders, 1922

Proclamation—A Warning to All Christians, 1923

Ecclesiastics Indicted, 1924

The Broadcaster, 1924

A Message of Hope, 1925

A Testimony to the Rulers of the World, 1926

Kingdom News No. 4 (Attempt to Wreck Garden Assembly—The Facts), 1939

Kingdom News No. 5 (Can Religion Save the World From Disaster?) 1939

It Must Be Stopped, 1940

Kingdom News No. 6 (Time of Darkness—Isaiah 60:2), 1940

Kingdom News No. 6 (London) (Which Will Give You Freedom? Religion or Christianity?), 1940

Kingdom News No. 7 (Do You Condemn or Wink at Unspeakable Crimes?), 1940

Kingdom News No. 8 (If the Bill Becomes Law), 1941

Kingdom News No. 9 (Victories in Your Defense), 1941

Kingdom News No. 9 (London) (Where Does the Church of Scotland Stand?), 1941

5

The Nathan H. Knorr Era
1942–1977

President
Born April 23, 1905
Died June 8, 1977

Periodicals

The Watchtower Announcing Jehovah's Kingdom
Nearly two hundred *Watchtower* magazine quotations that trace doctrinal changes through the Knorr era are included in my book *Index of Watchtower Errors* (Baker Book House, 1990).

Consolation, renamed *Awake!* in 1946
Offered from door to door along with *The Watchtower*, this magazine serves to draw the interest of nonreligious people with articles on nonbiblical subjects.

Informant, renamed *Kingdom Ministry* in 1956, *Our Kingdom Service* in 1976, and *Our Kingdom Ministry* in 1982
This members-only monthly publication features instructions for carrying on the house-to-house ministry,

as well as news about the organization's conventions and new publications.

The word *ministry* appeared in the title for twenty years, because the leadership taught that all Jehovah's Witnesses were ministers. In 1976 this teaching was reversed, and the word *ministry* removed. In 1982 the teaching was reversed again—back to the previous point of view—and the word *ministry* put back in.

Books

The New World, 1942

Although covering a wide range of topics, *The New World* is set up as a verse-by-verse commentary on the Book of Job.

The first book produced under the new policy of omitting the author's name, it also lacks the lively pugnacity that characterized most of J. F. Rutherford's works. It marks the beginning of a new era of upbeat but bland publications designed more as instructional textbooks for new members than as verbal assaults on those outside the organization.

This book also introduces the practice of depicting Jesus Christ in both sketches and full-color illustrations as a beardless adult (inside front and back covers, p. 88, opposite p. 97, and p. 252). The implication was not that he shaved his beard in violation of the Law of Moses (Lev. 19:27), but rather that a perfect man such as Christ would not have whiskers growing on his face. Watchtower publications continued to illustrate Jesus without facial hair for more than two decades, until this official statement finally appeared:

> Biblical evidence is the most reliable testimony to be found on this question, and a recent careful review of what it says indicates that Jesus did indeed have a beard. (The Watchtower, May 1, 1968, p. 286)

After that, Jesus' beard was restored.

The failure of J. F. Rutherford's prediction in *Millions Now Living Will Never Die* that Abraham, Isaac, and Jacob would return to life in 1925 resulted not in the sect's abandoning the idea but simply in advancing the date. Thus, *The New World* makes this prophecy on page 104:

> Those faithful men of old may be expected back from the dead any day now. . . .
>
> In this expectation the house at San Diego, California, which house has been much publicized with malicious intent by the religious enemy, was built, in 1930, and named "Beth-Sarim," meaning "House of the Princes." It is now held in trust for the occupancy of those princes on their return.

Page 130 adds that "the Scriptural and the physical facts prove that Job is due to be resurrected shortly with those faithful men and to appear on earth with them."

Bible, King James Version, 1942

Christians who accuse Jehovah's Witnesses of failing to use a "real" Bible are sometimes thrown off guard when the JWs display a King James Version printed by the Watchtower Society. Moreover, the Witnesses are prepared to defend most of their doctrines by using the King James Version, as they did for many years before publication of their New World Translation with its unique renderings. For help in answering JW misuse of Bible verses, please see my book *Jehovah's Witnesses Answered Verse by Verse* (Baker Book House, 1986).

"The Truth Shall Make You Free," 1943

This basic textbook of Watchtower theology is accompanied by a sixty-four-page booklet of study questions for use in individual or group study.

Perhaps of greatest interest in this volume is the chronology presented on page 152:

> From Adam's creation to the end of 1943 A.D. is 5,971 years. We are therefore near the end of six thousand years of human

history, with conditions upon us and tremendous events at hand foreshadowed by those of Noah's day.

This constitutes a major revision of Watchtower chronology, a departure from C. T. Russell's dating system, which had man's first six thousand years ending in 1874. In the 1960s the Society would begin emphasizing these calculations to raise apocalyptic expectations for the year 1975, similar to those entertained by Russell's predecessors, the Second Adventists, prior to 1874.

Also of interest is the assumption expressed on page 285 (1943 edition) that man would never get outside the earth's atmosphere:

> Man on earth can no more get rid of these demonic "heavens" than man can by airplane or rockets or other means get up above the air envelope which is about our earthly globe and in which man breathes. God alone can and will deliver humankind from such demon powers of control.

The Watchtower's assumption proved false as early as 1957, when the Soviet Union put its Sputnik satellite into orbit above the air envelope, and in the years since then when men themselves have ridden rockets above the atmosphere, even all the way to the moon and back.

"The Kingdom Is at Hand," 1944

Just two years after the practice of publishing books without an author's byline was instituted, this volume goes so far as to include a brief history of the Watchtower organization without mentioning the name of its founder:

> In July of A.D. 1879 a small but portentous publication began to appear. It was a magazine called *Zion's Watch Tower and Herald of Christ's Presence.* Its name spoke for it. The Christians back of this publication were consecrated persons that had separated themselves from all religious organizations of "Christendom" and heathendom.... Who the individuals were is unimportant; ... The same publishers of the magazine issued

in 1889 a book entitled "The Time Is at Hand", and in 1891
another book entitled "Thy Kingdom Come". (p. 310)

How strange that, less than thirty years after his death, C.
T. Russell should be transformed from "the special messenger to the last Age of the Church" (*The Finished Mystery*, p. 53) to a nameless individual whose identity is
"unimportant"!

Kingdom Service Song Book, 1944

Some years before this hymnal was produced, the
organization not only discarded the 1928 book called *Songs
of Praise to Jehovah* but also dispensed with singing at meetings entirely. But when this new collection of 62 songs was
released at a JW convention in August 1944, congregational
singing was reintroduced at the weekly service meetings.

"Now the brothers were happy to be able to sing
together again," comments *Jehovah's Witnesses in the
Divine Purpose* (p. 215). Indeed, the very fact that songs of
praise to God by thousands of people could be turned off
and on again at command from Brooklyn headquarters says
a lot about the regimentation of Jehovah's Witnesses.

The *Kingdom Service Song Book* is unique in that it
gives no credits to lyric writers or composers, a practice to
be followed from this time on in future songbooks. This
means, of course, that musical pieces requiring acknowl-
edgment or permission for use are no longer included. In
fact, more than a third of the songs featured here were written by Jehovah's Witnesses themselves.

Bible, American Standard Version, 1944

The reason the Watchtower Society would want to
publish an edition of the American Standard Version Bible
should be obvious:

The outstanding feature of merit of the *American Standard Version* is its consistent use of the memorial name JEHOVAH. This

> great name appears some 6,600 times in the Hebrew Scriptures,
> it being uniformly substituted for "LORD" and "GOD" (printed
> in capital and small capitals) as found in the Authorized Ver-
> sion. (*Theocratic Aid to Kingdom Publishers*, p. 278)

Jehovah's Witnesses switched briefly from the King James
Version to the American Standard Version prior to release
of their own New World Translation.

Theocratic Aid to Kingdom Publishers, 1945

This 382-page textbook was prepared for use in local
theocratic ministry school meetings that had been started
two years earlier with the ninety-six-page booklet *Course
in Theocratic Ministry* (see discussion). It provides instruction in study techniques, various aspects of public speaking, effective argumentation, as well as a history of religion
from the Watchtower Society's point of view. It is this training program, still in operation in Jehovah's Witness congregations today, that makes JWs such formidable foes in
doorstep debates.

However, this textbook also reveals one of Jehovah's
Witnesses' greatest weaknesses, their overconfidence in
their organization and virtual idolization of it:

> What is the channel used to beam forth the ever-increasing
> light? . . . The physical facts . . . reveal the light-channel to be
> the Watchtower Society. This Society is the only organization
> heralding earth-wide the enlightening announcement that the
> Kingdom is at hand, is here. (pp. 249–250)

Theocratic Aid to Kingdom Publishers was replaced
in 1955 with *Qualified to Be Ministers*.

"Equipped for Every Good Work," 1946

A supplementary textbook for the local congregation's
theocratic ministry school meeting, this volume outlines
the origin and history of the Bible and features a brief discussion of each book in the Old and New Testaments.

"Let God Be True," 1946

This book, including a revised edition released in 1952, served for many years as a basic textbook for new disciples, instructing them in the doctrines they must accept and practices they must adopt so they might be received for baptism by Jehovah's Witnesses. The 1952 second edition is revised throughout to employ terminology and direct quotations from the *New World Translation of the Christian Greek Scriptures.*

New World Translation of the Christian Greek Scriptures, 1950

Switching from the King James Version to the American Standard Version in 1944 was merely a stopgap measure. It enabled Jehovah's Witnesses to point to the name *Jehovah* throughout the Old Testament, but it did not let them find that name in the New Testament, nor did it solve the problem of Bible verses that plainly contradicted Watchtower teaching. The *New World Translation of the Christian Greek Scriptures* does both. It inserts the name *Jehovah* throughout the New Testament and it slants the rendering of many verses toward agreement with Watchtower doctrine.

Eventually appearing as part of a complete *New World Translation of the Holy Scriptures* from Genesis through Revelation, the New Testament was produced first, since that was the portion most in need of revision from a JW standpoint. Although hundreds of verses are changed to conform to Watchtower doctrine, almost all of these fall into three categories.

1. There are more than 230 insertions of *Jehovah,* in spite of the Society's admission that "no early surviving Greek manuscript of the 'New Testament' contains the personal name of God" (*The Watchtower,* March 1, 1991, p. 28). Where ancient manuscripts would normally be cited for support of such rendering, New World Translation footnote

symbols *J¹* through *J²¹* refer instead to much later *translations* of New Testament portions into Hebrew. For example, J¹ is a version titled *Matthew in Hebrew,* edited by J. Mercerus in Paris in 1555. J² is the Book of Matthew translated into Hebrew in 1385 by a Jew named Shem Tob as part of an attack he wrote against Christianity. J⁵ is a translation of the *Liturgical Gospels* into Hebrew in 1574 by a converted Jew named Frederick Petri, and J¹⁴ is a Hebrew translation by John Christian Reichardt of the entire New Testament, published in London in 1846.

But not all appearances of the word *Lord (kyrios)* are rendered "Jehovah" in the New World Translation. If, for example, the Watchtower Society had consistently followed its reference J¹⁴, then it would have translated 1 Corinthians 12:3 as "nobody can say: 'Jesus is Jehovah!' except by holy spirit." Instead, in this instance the New World Translation retains the customary rendering— "Jesus is Lord!"—since the Watchtower applies the name Jehovah only to God the Father.

The overall effect of the insertion of *Jehovah* in the *New World Translation of the Christian Greek Scriptures* is to Judaize the New Testament and to obscure the person and position of Jesus Christ. In some cases it totally changes the meaning of a text, such as Romans 14:8–9. With each appearance of a form of the Greek word *kyrios* emphasized, it reads this way in the American Standard Version:

> For whether we live, we live unto the *Lord;* or whether we die, we die unto the *Lord:* whether we live therefore, or die, we are the *Lord's.* For to this end Christ died and lived again, that he might be *Lord* of both the dead and the living (italics added).

The things said about the Lord in verse 8 are logically related to what follows in verse 9. But in the New World Translation the change of person creates a non sequitur:

> For both if we live, we live to *Jehovah,* and if we die, we die to *Jehovah.* Therefore both if we live and if we die, we belong to

Jehovah. For to this end Christ died and came to life again, that he might be *Lord* over both the dead and the living (italics added).

Verse 8 now speaks about Jehovah, whom JWs understand to be God the Father, while verse 9 speaks about someone else, namely Christ, whom they believe to be an angel—so verse 9 no longer follows logically from what precedes it, and the meaning of the passage is completely altered.

2. Other verses in the New World Translation are rendered in such a manner that they no longer appear to teach the deity of Christ or the personality of the Holy Spirit.

Thus *holy spirit* is written without the capitalization that is customary in English, in conformity with the Watchtower teaching that "it" is merely an impersonal force used by God. And where the American Standard Version has Jesus say, "Before Abraham was born, I am," at John 8:58, the New World Translation says, "Before Abraham came into existence, I have been." (Yet the literal Greek is shown to read *I am* in both the *Emphatic Diaglott* and the *Kingdom Interlinear Translation* published by the Watchtower Society.)

Perhaps the best-known verse in the New World Translation is John 1:1, which reads, "In [the] beginning[1] the Word was, and the Word was with God, and the Word was a god." (Compare, "the Word was God" in standard translations.) For many years the Watchtower Society cited in support of its "a god" rendering *The New Testament,* by Johannes Greber (1937), since Greber also translated: "the Word was a god." JW publications quote or cite Greber in support of this and other renderings, as follows:

Aid to Bible Understanding (1969), pages 1134 and 1669
"Make Sure of All Things—Hold Fast to What is Fine"
   (1965), page 489
The Watchtower, September 15, 1962, page 554
The Watchtower, October 15, 1975, page 640
The Watchtower, April 15, 1976, page 231

"The Word"—Who Is He? According To John (1962), page 5

However, after Christian countercult ministries gave considerable publicity to the fact that Greber was a spiritist who claimed that spirits showed him what words to use in his translation, *The Watchtower* of April 1, 1983, said on page 31:

> This translation was used occasionally in support of renderings of Matthew 27:52, 53 and John 1:1, as given in the *New World Translation* and other authoritative Bible versions. But as indicated in a foreword to the 1980 edition of *The New Testament* by Johannes Greber, this translator relied on "God's Spirit World" to clarify for him how he should translate difficult passages. It is stated: "His wife, a medium of God's Spiritworld was often instrumental in conveying the correct answers from God's Messengers to Pastor Greber." *The Watchtower* has deemed it improper to make use of a translation that has such a close rapport with spiritism. (Deut. 18:10–12) The scholarship that forms the basis for the rendering of the above-cited texts in the *New World Translation* is sound and for this reason does not depend at all on Greber's translation for authority. Nothing is lost, therefore, by ceasing to use his *New Testament*.

Thus, it appeared that the Society had only just now discovered Greber's spiritistic connections and immediately repented of using him for support. However, this was a deception, because the JW organization already knew of Greber's spiritism back in 1956. *The Watchtower* of February 15, 1956, contains nearly a full page devoted to warning readers against Johannes Greber and his translation. It refers to his book titled *Communication with the Spirit-World: Its Laws and Its Purposes* and states, "Very plainly the spirits in which ex-priest Greber believes helped him in his translation" (*The Watchtower,* February 15, 1956, p. 111).

3. Certain other verses that pertain neither to the name Jehovah nor to the subject of deity are given unusual ren-

derings in the New World Translation to support various other Watchtower doctrines. For example, the cross of Christ is replaced by a "torture stake" in Matthew 10:38 and elsewhere; rather than look forward to Christ's coming the apostles anticipate his "presence" in Matthew 24:3; and instead of being crucified Jesus is "impaled" in Luke 24:20 and throughout the Gospels.

Of the various revisions to the New World Translation over the years none have been of great doctrinal significance except that of 1971, which changed "let all God's angels worship him" in Hebrews 1:6 to say "let all God's angels do obeisance to him." (From 1879 through 1953 the Watchtower Society taught that Jesus should be worshiped. In 1954 the teaching was reversed, but the Bible verse was not altered to agree until 1971.)

The Watchtower Society has never disclosed the identities of the men of the secretive New World Translation committee, but former Governing Body member Raymond Franz identifies them in his book *Crisis of Conscience* as Nathan Knorr, Frederick Franz, Albert Schroeder, and George Gangas, of whom he indicates that only his uncle Fred had any qualifications: two years of Greek at the University of Cincinnati, plus self-taught Hebrew.

Some of the New World Translation's odd renderings are discussed in my book *Jehovah's Witnesses Answered Verse by Verse,* and a closer look at the Greek is provided in *The Jehovah's Witnesses' New Testament,* by Robert H. Countess.

"This Means Everlasting Life," 1950

This is a basic textbook that teaches the Watchtower's version of how to gain salvation and how to live a Christian life. Jehovah's Witnesses studied it in groups and also used it as a second study book for new converts who had already completed an introductory text.

Songs to Jehovah's Praise, 1950

Regarding this collection of ninety-one songs released at the Theocracy's Increase Assembly, *Jehovah's Witnesses in the Divine Purpose* makes this comment on the new songbook:

> [It] contained many more original compositions, written by Jehovah's Witnesses to express in words and music their way of worship, which was so completely different from anything known to apostate religion, a constant reminder in song of their exclusive place in the divine purpose. (p. 259)

For example, lyrics featuring language taken from the King James Bible are replaced with wording found in the Society's New World Translation, the New Testament portion of which was released that same year.

More than three million copies of this songbook were eventually distributed in eighteen languages.

What Has Religion Done for Mankind? 1951

Released at a Watchtower convention in Wembley Stadium, London, England, in August of 1951, the first edition of this book features before the title page a letter addressed to "Preachers of the Truth" signed by "THE PUBLISHERS." (Later editions omit the letter.) It tells them that "we as Jehovah's witnesses have a big work to do in straightening out this matter of religion in the minds of the people." This is ironic in view of the fact that it was only five months earlier that Jehovah's Witnesses themselves changed their view of religion when the *Watchtower* magazine of March 15, 1951, "approved of using the adjectives 'true' and 'false' respecting religion" (*1975 Yearbook of Jehovah's Witnesses,* p. 225). Prior to that they had used the word *religion* to mean only false worship, and JWs had paraded with signs proclaiming, "Religion Is a Snare and a Racket."

So, before they could offer to use this new book in teaching others—"straightening out this matter of religion

in the minds of the people"—Jehovah's Witnesses themselves had to read it first to straighten out in their own
minds their organization's new definition of religion.

The book first presents the history of true and false
religion, from the Watchtower's new viewpoint, tracing
religious developments from the Garden of Eden through
the Genesis flood, the Tower of Babel, and the rise and fall
of the nation of Israel. Then it looks briefly at Hinduism,
Buddhism, and Confucianism. Returning to the Bible, it
presents the Watchtower's version of the beginning of
Christianity, which is soon overshadowed by an apostate
Roman Catholic Church. After a brief look at Islam, it
returns to Christendom and dismisses the Protestant Reformation with the argument that it "was more a rebellion
against the religious supremacy of the pope than a real
reformation and a return to primitive Christianity" (p. 294).
Then it declares that all of Christendom rejected the kingdom of God when it was born in heaven in 1914. Only the
newly formed Watchtower organization recognized and
welcomed the birth of the kingdom. Soon God will destroy
all other religious groups, leaving only Jehovah's Witnesses
to carry on true worship, it concludes.

"Let God Be True" (revised edition), 1952

Please see the discussion of the 1946 edition.

New World Translation of the Hebrew Scriptures, Volume I, 1953

After release of the *New World Translation of the
Christian Greek Scriptures* in 1950, the Old Testament was
produced a portion at a time over the next ten years. Volume 1 includes Genesis through Ruth.

One need read only as far as Genesis 1:2 to observe
that the translation has been tailored to fit Watchtower doctrine. Instead of God's Spirit moving upon the face of the
waters, the New World Translation says, "God's active force
was moving to and fro over the surface of the waters." This

rendering conforms to the Jehovah's Witness view of the Holy Spirit as an impersonal force rather than deity.

"Make Sure of All Things," 1953

The title page declares that this is "a compilation of scriptures from the Holy Bible under seventy main headings to enable the searcher for truth to ascertain the fundamental doctrines and be assured thereof." The implication is that the Scriptures themselves teach these doctrines. But the selection of verses out of context, the arrangement of strings of unrelated verses, and the comments employed in introducing them can greatly affect the doctrines derived.

Consider, for example, the section titled "Blood Transfusion." It features this subsection employing verses from the American Standard Version:

> **Blood Not to Be Stored**
> **Deut. 12:16** "Ye shall not eat the blood; thou shalt pour it out upon the earth as water."
> **Lev. 17:13** "Whatsoever man there be of the children of Israel, or of the strangers that sojourn among them, who taketh in hunting any beast or bird that may be eaten; he shall pour out the blood thereof, and cover it with dust."

The implication is that it is wrong to store human blood in a blood bank for medical use in treating sick or injured people. That interpretation is erroneous for these reasons: (1) The contexts of both verses reveal that the Bible is discussing what to do with the blood of animals slaughtered for food, not human blood; (2) the contexts of both verses discuss the placing of blood from slaughtered domestic animals on the altar at the tabernacle of worship (Deut. 12:27; Lev. 17:11); and (3) rather than prohibit the storing of donated human blood in a refrigerated blood bank, the verses quoted tell the Jews how to dispose of the blood of animals that are either wild animals unsuitable for sacrifice under Jewish law or domestic animals slaughtered at home and hence at a considerable distance from the tabernacle and its altar. The blood of edible animals belonged to God; if unable to place it on his altar, the Jew was to pour it out on the ground.

In similar fashion *"Make Sure of All Things"* assembles groups of verses to "prove" such points as "Only-begotten Son the First Creation" (p. 79), "Jesus Was Put to Death on a Simple Upright Stake . . . Not a Cross" (p. 84), "Divine Physical Healing Not Experienced Today" (p. 149), "One's birthday . . . not to be commemorated" (p. 166), "The [Christmas] 'star' was a light Satan used to guide astrologers (demon worshipers) in his scheme to locate Jesus for destruction by Herod" (p. 167), and "Only 144,000 Followers of Christ Will Go to Heaven" (p. 196).

Worthy of note is the fact that this is the last Watchtower book to declare "Christ to Be Worshiped" (p. 85). Although taught since 1879, the organization reversed the doctrine in 1954, thus prohibiting worship of Christ.[2] Nevertheless, the expression "Christ to Be Worshiped" still appears in a subheading on page 85 in the 1957 revised edition. It is eliminated in the more thorough revision retitled *"Make Sure of All Things: Hold Fast to What Is Fine"* and released in 1965 (see discussion).

"New Heavens and a New Earth," 1953

The first edition (2 million copies) differs from later printings in that it features before the title page a one-page letter from "The Publishers" dated July 25, 1953, and addressed "To the New World Society." The first edition was released on that date at a convention of Jehovah's Witnesses in New York City, and the New World Society is a collective name for Jehovah's Witnesses themselves, indicating that they expect to make up the nucleus of the "new heavens and a new earth" spoken of in the book's title.

How does the Watchtower Society interpret this expression taken from Isaiah 66:22? The book does not come to the point quickly, but on page 228 it says that "the birth of the Kingdom in 1914 (A.D.) denoted the introduction of new heavens," that is, Christ's heavenly government. Similarly, the new earth is identified as a new human society living on this planet under God's rulership. Moreover, "It is solely in brotherly association with the New World society that we can possibly survive when this old world passes away" (p. 363). So, one must become a Jehovah's Witness to live in the new world.

New World Translation of the Hebrew Scriptures, Volume II, 1955

After release of the *New World Translation of the Christian Greek Scriptures* in 1950, the Old Testament was produced a portion at a time over the next ten years. Volume 2 includes 1 Samuel through Esther.

Qualified to Be Ministers, 1955

This book took the place of *Theocratic Aid to Kingdom Publishers* as the primary text for the theocratic ministry school meeting in local Jehovah's Witness congregations. It features instruction in public speaking, methods for personal study, techniques for house-to-house ministry, and directions for congregation meetings. It also contains lessons on the history of religion and a "Modern History of Jehovah's Witnesses."

Quite revealing is the book's interpretation of the statement at 1 Corinthians 13:7 that love "believes all things":

> If we have love for Jehovah and for the organization of his people we shall not be suspicious, but shall, as the Bible says, "believe all things," all the things that *The Watchtower* brings out. (p. 156)

A 1967 revision of *Qualified to Be Ministers* replaces the history of Jehovah's Witnesses with chapters on "Progressive Speech Training" that accompany a speech counsel slip, or report card, to be marked by the instructor after a student delivers a talk in the school.

You May Survive Armageddon Into God's New World, 1955

This book presents the Watchtower Society's interpretation of biblical end-times prophecies, with primary focus on the sect's teaching that the "great crowd" of believers will not go to heaven but rather will live forever on earth. As summed up on page 367, there are "42 types and prophecies of the earthly heirs of the New World" discussed throughout the book. These include King Hiram's woodcutters, Rebekah's nurse Deborah, King Saul's son Jonathan, the queen of Sheba, Naaman the Syrian, Judge Jephthah's daughter, and the prodigal son of Jesus' parable—all of whom allegedly prefigure such a secondary class of believers outside the body of Christ, without a heavenly hope.

Faith on the March, by A. H. Macmillan (Englewood Cliffs: Prentice-Hall, Inc.), 1957

Not actually published by the Watchtower Society, but written by its vice president and prefaced with an introduction by president N. H. Knorr, this history of Jehovah's Witnesses is more than just quasi-official. It is really a Watchtower publication printed by an outside firm, perhaps to gain acceptance in bookstores and public libraries. Lacking the frank evenhandedness of an objective history, the work is an obviously one-sided advertisement for Jehovah's Witnesses aimed at presenting the Watchtower Society as the "one channel" God uses to "reveal his purposes" to mankind (p. 137).

With this in mind, the reader who is careful to consult outside sources as well can still derive a lot of useful information from Macmillan. He includes a chapter detailing Charles Taze Russell's involvement with the Second Adventists and the split that led to formation of a breakaway sect led by Russell. But his first-person accounts also shed light on matters not illuminated elsewhere.

Of particular interest, for example, is his story of what occurred when following J. F. Rutherford's instructions, he used the police to break up a meeting of the Society's board of directors. Four of the seven directors were opposed to Rutherford. So, when they called a meeting of the board at the Watchtower's Hicks Street office in Brooklyn, Macmillan sent office manager Robert J. Martin after a policeman. In came a typical old Irish boy in blue, an acquaintance of both Martin and Macmillan, who twirled his nightstick and, in a thick Irish accent, ordered the four directors to leave the building (p. 79). This incident reveals the bitterness and hostility that existed at that time among the men who made up what Jehovah's Witnesses today call their Governing Body, as well as the sort of political maneuvering and "dirty tricks" that helped determine who would eventually control the vast Watchtower empire.

Since *Faith on the March* appears to be aimed at the general public, it was supplemented rather than supplanted by *Jehovah's Witnesses in the Divine Purpose,* published two years later for study by JWs themselves.

New World Translation of the Hebrew Scriptures, Volume III, 1957

After release of the *New World Translation of the Christian Greek Scriptures* in 1950, the Old Testament was produced a portion at a time over the next ten years. Volume 3 includes Job through The Song of Solomon.

New World Translation of the Hebrew Scriptures, Volume IV, 1958

After release of the *New World Translation of the Christian Greek Scriptures* in 1950, the Old Testament was produced a portion at a time over the next ten years. Volume 4 includes Isaiah through Lamentations.

Branch Office Procedure of the Watch Tower Bible and Tract Society of Pennsylvania, 1958

Although separate legal entities, the various Watchtower corporations around the world function as branches of the Pennsylvania corporation, which serves as the parent body. This internal handbook was issued to the men involved in operating the branch offices.

From Paradise Lost to Paradise Regained, 1958

Written in simple language, set in large bold sans serif type, and abundantly illustrated, this volume is designed for children and new readers. Beginning with the sect's interpretation of the creation account and concluding with a restored earthly paradise, it presents a comprehensive overview of Watchtower beliefs. In the concluding chapter it states plainly that "only the preachers of God's kingdom can expect to be protected during the end of this world and to live through Armageddon into the new world" (p. 249).

A whole generation of Jehovah's Witness children were frightened by the illustrations of Armageddon on pages 208 and 209. Drawn with "soul-chilling terror" on their faces, youngsters are shown fleeing in panic as buildings topple and burn; then they are shown falling into huge crevasses as the earth opens up beneath their feet, swallowing up screaming children together with their toy dolls, bicycles, and pet dogs.

The abundant pictures of Jesus Christ are also of interest, as he is portrayed without facial hair. Illustrations of a beardless Jesus characterize Watchtower publications during the period from 1942 through early 1968 (see the discussion of *The New World,* 1942).

"Your Will Be Done on Earth," 1958

Interpreting the "beasts" in Daniel and Revelation as symbolic of world powers, this book examines world history in the light of Bible prophecy and then goes on to present the Watchtower Society's scenario of end-times events. It concentrates heavily on the struggle between "the king of the south" and "the king of the north" in Daniel, chapter 11, identifying the modern king of the south as "Britain and America" (p. 263) and the king of the north as "the Soviet Union, the Communist power that, since it seized power in Russia in 1917, has held world domination as its aim to this day" (p. 278). The book prophesies that "down to the 'time of the end' at Armageddon there will be competitive coexistence between the 'two kings'" (p. 297), that is, between the Soviet Union and the British-American combine, and that "Jehovah's angel foretold further aggressions by the Communist king of the north before his end in Armageddon" (p. 300). However, as things actually turned out, the early 1990s saw the collapse of the communist empire and the dissolution of the Soviet Union, in spite of the Watchtower Society's prediction that a Communist Soviet Union would continue until Armageddon.

On page 371 there is a useful list of "Prophetic 'times' and 'days'" showing clearly and concisely the Watchtower Society's egocentric interpretation of Daniel's prophecies:

> "TIMES, TWO TIMES, AND HALF A TIME" (Daniel 7:25; 12:7, RS):
> Began in first half of November, 1914
> Ended May 7, 1918, at arrest of Watch Tower Society's officers and companions
> (Compare the 42 months of Revelation 11:2)
> "A THOUSAND TWO HUNDRED AND NINETY DAYS" (Daniel 12:11, Le):
> Began the end of January, 1919
> Ended the first half of September, 1922, at the second Cedar Point (Ohio) convention
> "THE THOUSAND THREE HUNDRED AND THIRTY-FIVE DAYS" (Daniel 12:12, AT):
> Began the first half of September, 1922, at the second Cedar Point (Ohio) convention
> Ended in the month of May, 1926, at the London (England) International Convention

"TWO THOUSAND AND THREE HUNDRED EVENINGS AND
MORNINGS" (Daniel 8:14, *RS*):
> Began in the month of May, 1926, at the London (England)
> International Convention (May 25–31)
> Ended on October 15, 1932, with the official publication of
> notice in *The Watchtower*

Jehovah's Witnesses in the Divine Purpose, 1959

This is the most complete history of itself that the
Watchtower organization has ever published. But it is also
extremely one-sided and should not be relied on exclusively
without consulting more objective accounts. For example,
it states that "Jehovah's witnesses are the most ancient religious group . . . whose history runs farther back than any
religious denomination" (p. 8), whereas independent historians date the sect from 1879 when Charles Taze Russell
began publishing *Zion's Watch Tower and Herald of Christ's
Presence.* Of course, when it goes on to indicate that "Jesus'
disciples were all Jehovah's witnesses too" (p. 9), it becomes
clear that the sect is simply laying claim to those it consid-
ers to be true worshipers in prior centuries.

Although this account fills more than three hundred
two-column pages, it is presented in the form of a con-
versation between a JW couple, John and Maria, and their
non-Witness neighbors Tom and Lois. The latter keep asking questions that move the former to provide all the
information.

Even this history, full of self-commendation, at times
proves embarrassing to today's Watchtower Society, since
some of the doctrinal changes it reports as "increasing light"
(p. 100) have since been reversed. For example, the book
says this about the years following the First World War:

> There were many false doctrines and practices that had not yet
> been cleaned out of the organization. . . . With considerable
> misunderstanding they had accepted earthly political govern-
> ments as the "superior authorities" that God had ordained

> according to Romans 13:1; and as a result the Witnesses had
> been held in fear of man, particularly the civil rulers. (p. 91)

But, after identifying these "higher powers" as God and
Christ, and teaching this for some years, the leadership
later reversed the teaching again and returned to the former view held during and immediately after the First World
War, namely that Romans 13:1 speaks of earthly political
governments. Thus the current teaching is labeled a false
doctrine in this history.

Thus, too, the historical record presented here belies
the organization's current claim that it has never reinstated
former teachings after it rejected them:

> At times explanations given by Jehovah's visible organization
> have shown adjustments, seemingly to previous points of view.
> But this has not actually been the case. (*The Watchtower,*
> December 1, 1981, p. 27)

Yet, it is obviously the case in the matter of the interpretation of Romans 13:1. The original teaching was once again
adopted after years of being called a false doctrine.

While doctrinal changes have resulted in many Watchtower publications contradicting one another over the
years, it seldom occurs that one of the Society's books will
contradict itself internally. *Jehovah's Witnesses in the
Divine Purpose* is an exception. On page 63 it asserts that
Jehovah's Witnesses "have never published a biography of
Pastor Russell." But on pages 16–17 it quotes from "his
biography as published" in the foreword of the 1926 edition of *The Divine Plan of the Ages.*

Instead of *Jehovah's Witnesses in the Divine Purpose,*
the history more apt to be referenced by Jehovah's Witnesses today is that found in the *1975 Yearbook of Jehovah's Witnesses.* Persons who seek an account that is not
slanted in favor of the organization will benefit from reading *Apocalypse Delayed: The Story of Jehovah's Witnesses,*
by M. James Penton.

New World Translation of the Hebrew Scriptures, Volume V, 1960

After release of the *New World Translation of the Christian Greek Scriptures* in 1950, the Old Testament was produced a portion at a time over the next ten years. This final installment includes Ezekiel through Malachi.

Kingdom Ministry School Course, 1960

This instructional manual for congregation elders served as the textbook for a course training them to carry out their various duties.

New World Translation of the Holy Scriptures, 1961

The New Testament and Old Testament installments released beginning in 1950 were revised and combined into this one-volume Bible. Please see the discussions under *New World Translation of the Christian Greek Scriptures* (1950) and *New World Translation of the Hebrew Scriptures, Volume I* (1953).

Several new editions have been published over the years featuring different type sizes, bindings, marginal notes, footnotes, maps, and appendix articles. A second revision to the text itself was released in 1970, a third in 1971, and a fourth in 1984. The only revision of major doctrinal significance was the change made in 1971 at Hebrews 1:6, where the rendering was changed from "let all God's angels worship him" to read "let all God's angels do obeisance to him." (From 1879 through 1953 the Watchtower Society taught that Jesus should be worshiped. In 1954 the teaching was reversed, but the Bible verse was not altered to agree until the revision of 1971.)

As of this writing the New World Translation has also been published in nine other European languages and in Japanese. These foreign editions, however, are translations from English rather than from the original Bible languages. The combined total number of copies printed to date is approximately 60 million.

"Let Your Name Be Sanctified," 1961

This book focuses attention on the name Jehovah, of central importance to Jehovah's Witnesses. Much of the book is devoted to a discussion of the books 1 and 2 Kings, particularly the roles of Elijah and Elisha. It presents Elijah as prefiguring the Watchtower Society's leadership and activities through the presidency of J. F. Rutherford, and Elisha as prefiguring the same after Rutherford's death:

> But on Thursday, January 8, 1942, Rutherford died at seventy-two years of age. . . . As viewed from our present time, it appears that there the Elijah work passed, to be succeeded by the Elisha work. (p. 336)

> The anointed Elisha class undertook the responsibility of carrying out fully the divine commission as symbolized by Elijah's official garment. Five days after Rutherford's death the boards of directors of the Watch Tower corporations for New York and Pennsylvania held a joint meeting and unanimously elected N. H. Knorr, one of the anointed remnant, to be president of both corporations of the Society. (p. 338)

Watch Tower Publications Index (1930–1960), 1961

A cumulative index of *The Watchtower,* as well as of *The Golden Age, Consolation,* and *Awake!* magazines, this *Index* also references the contents of thirty-four books and eighty-three booklets published during the years covered.

Although the foreword cautions users to be "guided by the more recent references cited, since there has been much advancement over the years in the understanding of many Bible truths" (p. 5), it fails to mention that some of the more embarrassing references are omitted entirely. For example, under "Vaccinations, Bible view" there are only two citations: *The Watchtower,* 1958, page 575, and 1952, page 764. Looking up the 1952 reference we find this view concerning vaccination: "After consideration of the matter, it does not appear to us to be in violation of the everlasting covenant made with Noah." Completely omitted is any reference to *The Golden Age* of February 4, 1931, page 293, where the opposite is stated, namely that "vaccination is a direct violation of the everlasting covenant that God made with Noah."

The selection of 1930 as the earliest publication year to include in the *Index* was no doubt due to similar considerations. For example, under "Dates of Prophetic Significance" there is no listing for 1874, although the organization's books published as late as 1929 gave that as the date of Christ's invisible return. The 1930 cutoff also eliminates all the references to the Great Pyramid of Egypt that had served as a basis for chronological calculations throughout the sect's first half century. And it conveniently leaves behind the failed prophecies predicting amazing events for the year 1925.

So, even in a publication as straightforward as an index, there is a certain amount of manipulation of information to preserve the image the Watchtower Society wishes to project.

Please see, also, *Watch Tower Publications Index (1930–1985)*, 1986.

"All Scripture Is Inspired of God and Beneficial," 1963

Written primarily for Jehovah's Witnesses themselves to use in conjunction with their weekly Theocratic Ministry School meetings, this is a commentary on the entire Bible. The first 270 pages consist of a brief discussion of each Bible book in terms of authorship and significance, plus a summary of the book's contents. The remaining eighty pages of *"All Scripture Is Inspired of God and Beneficial"* touch on Bible geography, chronology, and archaeology, the Bible canon, Greek and Hebrew texts, and various English language translations. An entire chapter is devoted to "Advantages of the 'New World Translation.'"

This book figured prominently in an incident leading up to my own departure from Jehovah's Witnesses in 1982 after I had spent thirteen years as an active member. Besides being of personal importance, this episode also sheds light on how JWs view their literature and the Bible.

As one of the elders in the local congregation I had been assigned to give a fifteen-minute instruction talk, the chief discourse at the Thursday night Theocratic Ministry School meeting. My talk was to be on the Book of Zechariah, using material from *"All Scripture Is Inspired of God and Beneficial"*—a routine lecture. By this time, however, I had come to realize the importance of going to the Bible itself, rather than to Watchtower literature, to find real truth. Yet, I knew from experience that most of the Witnesses in my audience who had done their homework prior to my talk had read the commentary but had not bothered to read the Book of Zechariah itself. So, in the course of my lecture I called attention to this fact and then admonished the audience, "Since the Bible is the inspired Word of God, eternal and unchangeable, while *The Watchtower* is uninspired and has made many mistakes over the years that have required correction and readjustment, you would make the best use of your time by reading the Bible itself rather than reading Watchtower material." The usual stirring and whispering in the kingdom hall stopped, and one could have heard a pin drop as the audience sat stunned for the conclusion of my talk while I reiterated and drove home the point. What I had said, of course, violated the strictest of taboos, and that was the last time I was ever allowed to speak.

"All Scripture Is Inspired of God and Beneficial" was released again in 1990, completely retypeset but with the text essentially unchanged except for some updating and the addition of a few illustrations.

"Babylon the Great Has Fallen!" God's Kingdom Rules!
1963

This commentary covers Revelation, chapters 14–22, as well as portions of Isaiah, Jeremiah, and Daniel. Although offered on occasion to the public, it was written primarily for the Witnesses to study at their Tuesday night congregation book study meeting. They regarded it with reverence, believing it provided insight into some of the deeper truths of Bible prophecy on the end times.

The book identifies "Babylon the Great" of Revelation 17:5 as "the world empire of Babylonish religion" (p. 582) that embraces all religious organizations other than Jehovah's Witnesses:

> Just so, the member religious organizations of Babylon the Great are her children, her daughters born as a result of her fornication; and all these daughter systems are harlot organizations also. . . .
>   . . . she has drunk her fill "with the blood of the witnesses of Jesus." She has done this in her fanatical effort to deaden the voices of these witnesses who are preaching Jehovah's Messianic kingdom. (pp. 582–583)

What, then, about Revelation 14:8, which says, "And another, a second angel, followed, saying: 'She has fallen! Babylon the Great has fallen'" (NWT)? When is this verse fulfilled? The book answers that "she fell in the spring of the year 1919," when "in March of 1919 the prison doors were forced open to Jehovah's witnesses, and out they came and stayed out" (pp. 504–505). (See our discussion of *The Finished Mystery,* 1917, for details on the imprisonment of J. F. Rutherford and other Watchtower leaders during World War I.) So, the 704-page book *"Babylon the Great Has Fallen!" God's Kingdom Rules!* takes its title from a striking Bible verse that was allegedly fulfilled when the Watchtower organization scored a legal victory over its opponents.

The book was reprinted, essentially unchanged, in a 1981 edition.

"Make Sure of All Things; Hold Fast to What Is Fine," 1965

This is a major revision of the 1953 book with the shorter title *"Make Sure of All Things."* Many more subjects are discussed, and the volume is one hundred pages longer. The most important change from a doctrinal stand-point is the elimination of the teaching that Christ is to be worshiped.

"*Make Sure of All things; Hold Fast to What Is Fine*" was replaced in 1985 by *Reasoning from the Scriptures.*

"*Things in Which It Is Impossible for God to Lie,*" 1965

This book served as the initial text used to indoctri-nate prospective converts until 1968, when it was replaced in that function by *The Truth That Leads to Eternal Life,* a book both smaller and easier to understand. Thereafter, "*Things in Which It Is Impossible for God to Lie*" was often used as a second text that new converts would study after completing the first.

In spite of its strange title, "*Things in Which It Is Impossible for God to Lie*" is rather basic in its content. Beginning with arguments for God's existence and proofs that the Bible, rather than any other sacred book, is his word to mankind, it goes on to present the elements of Watchtower theology and end-times chronology. Then it concludes by telling readers what they must do to "inherit the earthly realm of the heavenly kingdom" (p. 406).

Life Everlasting—In Freedom of the Sons of God, 1966

Intended for study by Witnesses themselves or by advanced students near the point of baptism, this volume takes a much closer look at baptism and Christ's role as Savior. It also discusses church government, marriage, the JW's relationship to secular authorities, and the necessity of abstaining from military service and from blood trans-fusions.

Perhaps of greatest significance today is the fact that *Life Everlasting—In Freedom of the Sons of God* began in 1966 to focus attention on the year 1975 as the likely time for the end of this world and the beginning of Christ's mil-lennial reign:

According to this trustworthy Bible chronology six thousand years from man's creation will end in 1975, and the seventh period of a thousand years of human history will begin in the fall of 1975 C.E. . . . It would not be by mere chance or accident but would be according to the loving purpose of Jehovah God for the reign of Jesus Christ, the "Lord of the sabbath," to run parallel with the seventh millennium of man's existence. (pp. 29–30)

This book also clearly states the Watchtower's teaching that the "great crowd" of believers "will not be justified or declared righteous . . . by faith in Christ's blood" (p. 391). Instead, "eventually . . . they will be able to stand before the God of holiness on the basis of their own righteousness" (p. 392). And then, finally, after the devil's defeat at the end of Christ's millennial reign "Jehovah God will justify, declare righteous, on the basis of their own merit all perfected humans who have withstood that final, decisive test of mankind" (p. 400).

"Singing and Accompanying Yourselves With Music in Your Hearts," 1966

According to the announcement in the May, 15, 1966, *Watchtower* magazine, this new songbook was produced because "with the ever-increasing light there are new truths, new themes, clearer understanding and change of emphasis" (p. 313). Thus a conscious effort was made to eliminate any remaining melodies borrowed from traditional Christian hymns. Lyrics, too, were revamped to make them uniquely suited to the sect. Consider, for example, this chorus from the stirring march titled, "We Are Jehovah's Witnesses."

> We're Jehovah's witnesses;[3]
> We speak out in fearlessness!
> Ours is the God of true prophecy;
> What he foretells comes to be!

Such powerful musical propaganda stirs the emotions and thus enables many Witnesses to deny the factual evidence that their organization has achieved notoriety through repeated false prophecies; what it foretold for the years 1914, 1925, and 1975 certainly did not come to be.

Did Man Get Here by Evolution or by Creation? 1967

In a few pocket-size pages this small book assembles powerful biblical and scientific arguments against the theory of evolution and backs up those arguments with 248 footnoted references to scholarly and other outside sources. However, it leads the reader from rejecting evolution to accepting the Watchtower's teaching that Christ returned invisibly in 1914: "The beginning of the 'last days' in 1914 coincided with the invisible presence of Jesus Christ in Kingdom power" (p. 174). And it predicts that "thus the generation living in 1914 can expect to see the end of this wicked system of things" (p. 171).

Qualified to Be Ministers (revised), 1967

This revision of the 1955 book by the same title replaces its history of Jehovah's Witnesses with chapters on "Progressive Speech Training" that accompany a speech counsel slip, or report card, marked by their instructor after a student delivers a talk in the school.

"Your Word Is a Lamp to My Foot," 1967

This hardcover organizational manual took the place of the 1960 booklet *Preaching and Teaching in Peace and Unity.* Besides instructions for meetings and door-to-door literature distribution, it also features thirty-three pages of questions and answers for baptismal candidates. In other words, it is a Jehovah's Witness catechism, although JWs would recoil at the use of this word.

The *Lamp* book, as Witnesses call it, was replaced in 1972 by *Organization for Kingdom-Preaching and Disciple-Making.*

The Truth That Leads to Eternal Life, 1968

This powerful pocket-size publication was used as the initial study text for new converts until 1982, and it is probably responsible for bringing more people into the Watchtower organization than any other single publication— "over one million [members] being added to our ranks," according to *Our Kingdom Ministry* (September 1982, p. 4). The book itself was listed in the *1982 Guinness Book of Records* under "Highest Printings," and *Awake!* magazine reports that "by the first part of 1982, the printing of this Bible study aid had reached 102 million in 116 languages" (April 22, 1982, p. 29).

Written both fluently and concisely, the *Truth* book, as Witnesses refer to it, argues persuasively that paradise is soon to be restored earthwide and that the only survivors into that new world will be those who leave the false churches and join Jehovah's Witnesses.

A revised edition was released quietly in 1981. Why? Evidently because the nearly 100 million copies printed prior to that said this on page 9:

> Also, as reported back in 1960, a former United States Secretary of State, Dean Acheson, declared that our time is "a period of unequaled instability, unequaled violence." And he warned: "I know enough of what is going on to assure you that, in fifteen years from today, this world is going to be too dangerous to live in."

Fifteen years from 1960 was, of course, 1975, the year pointed to in other Watchtower Society books and magazines as the likely time for Armageddon and the end of the world. So, the Dean Acheson quotation served as independent confirmation that the world could not possibly continue beyond 1975. But, by 1981 this reference proved more embarrassing than helpful, and a revised edition of the *Truth* book was printed with this portion rewritten as follows:

Also, as reported back in 1960, a former United States Secretary of State, Dean Acheson, declared that our time is "a period
of unequaled instability, unequaled violence." Based on what
he knew was then going on in the world, it was his conclusion
that soon "this world is going to be too dangerous to live in."

On pages 88 and 89 of the original edition there appears
an even more damaging reference to "the book entitled
'Famine—1975!'" quoting its prediction: "By 1975 civil
disorder, anarchy, military dictatorships, runaway inflation, transportation breakdowns and chaotic unrest will be
the order of the day in many of the hungry nations." In the
1981 revision this embarrassing prediction about 1975 was
replaced by quotes from other sources that speak of famine
in more general terms.

Preparation of the book *You Can Live Forever in Paradise on Earth,* to be released in 1982 as a replacement for
the *Truth* book, must have already been under way in 1981,
but the Society evidently wanted to be able to refer back
to an edition of the *Truth* book that did not contain the
embarrassing allusions to 1975, and so it released this revision just before the book itself became obsolete.

The Kingdom Interlinear Translation of the Greek Scrip-
tures, 1969

Benjamin Wilson's *Emphatic Diaglott* proved an effective tool in the hands of Watchtower apologists from the
time of C. T. Russell onward. But its renderings did not
agree fully with the New World Translation, most notably
in the matter of the Society's insertion of the name *Jehovah* throughout the New Testament. (*Jehovah* appears in
the *Diaglott* at Matthew 21:9 and in seventeen other
places—far short of its more than 230 occurrences in the
New World Translation.) So, *The Kingdom Interlinear
Translation of the Greek Scriptures* was produced. It features the Westcott and Hort Greek text, with a literal Eng-

lish translation below each word, and the New World Translation in a parallel column.

Jehovah's Witness laborers and housewives who have no formal training in biblical Greek, but who have been instructed in the use of the *The Kingdom Interlinear Translation,* often come across as language scholars when making their rehearsed presentation on the doorstep. But, with a little study and preparation, Christians can turn the tables on them. For example, it is possible to point out that although the New World Translation column renders Jesus' words at John 8:58 as, "Most truly I say to YOU, Before Abraham came into existence, *I have been*" (emphasis added), the literal interlinear reading shows Jesus said, "I am." And, although *The Watchtower* of July 1, 1986, quotes an authority to establish that "the title *ho theos* [the God, or God] . . . is not applied in the N[ew] T[estament] to Jesus" (p. 31), *The Kingdom Interlinear Translation* at John 20:28 belies this statement by showing that the Greek for *ho theos* and the literal translation "the God" does apply to Jesus.

In 1985 a revised edition of *The Kingdom Interlinear Translation of the Greek Scriptures* was released. Please see the discussion in our next chapter.

Aid to Bible Understanding (A–Exodus), 1969

This initial portion of the Watchtower Society's first Bible dictionary was released two years prior to the complete volume that covered A–Z. Please see the discussion under *Aid to Bible Understanding,* 1971.

Is the Bible Really the Word of God? 1969

Reasoning logically so as to convince even the skeptic, this book advances excellent arguments in support of the divine inspiration of the Scriptures. But then, after building faith in the Bible, it attacks all other religious organizations and asserts that "Christendom's churches cannot escape being classified as part of the harlot-like 'Babylon the Great,'" and therefore "you cannot look to Christendom for guidance concerning His Word nor for an example of what its teachings and principles are" (p. 179). Instead, it invites the reader to contact Jehovah's Witnesses to receive free weekly Bible instruction in the home (p. 189).

Unlike most Watchtower books, *Is the Bible Really the Word of God?* does not feature questions at the bottom of each page. A separate study questions booklet was made available, primarily with a view toward using the book as a text for the congregation book study meeting, but also to facilitate its use in home study with interested individuals.

In 1989 this book was replaced by an abundantly illustrated volume titled, *The Bible—God's Word or Man's?*

"Then Is Finished the Mystery of God," 1969

This commentary covers the first thirteen chapters of Revelation but does not take them in numerical order. First, chapters 4–6, and chapter 7 through verse 8, are discussed; then, chapters 1–3; and finally, chapter 7 verse 9 through chapter 13. This unusual sequence evidently facilitates the interpretation of the prophecies in these chapters as having fulfillment upon the Watchtower Society during the years following 1914.

The title of this volume naturally calls to mind *The Finished Mystery* published by the Watchtower Society in 1917, but this comment explains the difference:

> In course of time *The Finished Mystery* proved to be unsatisfactory, because it had been written and published before many critical parts of the book of Revelation were fulfilled to make possible a correct understanding. (p. 252)

What, then, were the fulfillments of Revelation that took place between publication of *The Finished Mystery* in 1917 and *Then Is Finished the Mystery of God* in 1969, so that the latter might be able to record those fulfillments? The alleged fulfillments read much like a history of the Watchtower Bible and Tract Society. For example, the account of seven angels blowing seven trumpets in Revelation, chapters 8 through 11, is said to prophesy the Society's passing resolutions and distributing literature during the 1920s:

> When "the seven angels" of heaven prepared to blow the "seven trumpets" after the eighth angel had taken action, as described in Revelation 8:1–6, the anointed remnant of Kingdom heirs on earth for whom the angels are "spirits for public service" became involved. . . . They must proclaim the meaning of what the apostle John saw happen in symbols after each trumpet blast. (p. 214)

Each trumpet blast had a separate fulfillment:

> The Indictment also went out through the columns of *The Watch Tower* in its issue of September 1, 1924. That was only a beginning of the proclamation of the things that were disclosed after the trumpet blast by the third heavenly angel. (p. 226)

> As can be appreciated today, under the guidance of the fourth heavenly angel a regional convention of the International Bible Students Association was held in Indianapolis, Indiana, U.S.A., August 24–31, 1925. (p. 228)

And so on throughout the book, the blowing of the seven trumpets, the opening of the seven seals, and most of the other dramatic events described in Revelation are all shown to have their fulfillment in the twentieth-century Watchtower organization.

New World Translation of the Holy Scriptures (revised), 1970

Please see the discussion of the 1961 edition elsewhere in this chapter.

Aid to Bible Understanding (complete), 1971

Two years after the A-Exodus portion was made available separately, this complete Bible dictionary was released as a single volume of 1696 large pages. Its foreword declares

that some 250 researchers worked on the project over a
period of five years, but, as with other post-Rutherford publications, no names are listed. According to former Governing Body member Raymond Franz, nephew of President
Frederick W. Franz, 90 percent of the material originally
submitted was not used, because the 250 "researchers" who
prepared it had been selected on the basis of rank in the
organization's hierarchy rather than with regard to any abil-
ity as writers or proximity to research facilities. In his book
Crisis of Conscience (Atlanta: Commentary Press, 1983)
Raymond Franz reveals that he and four other headquarters workers, whom he names, actually did the bulk of the
writing and editing (pp. 20–21).

Its foreword also states that "*Aid to Bible Understanding* is not intended to be a doctrinal commentary or an inter-
pretative work" (p. 6). However, although this book does
avoid some of the more extreme prophetic speculation and
egocentric interpretation found in many JW publications,
it does present doctrines and slant interpretations to support Watchtower teachings. For example, the entry under
the heading "Cross" says simply, "See Torture Stake," since
Jehovah's Witnesses are taught that Jesus died on an upright
pole, not on a cross. And the dictionary's articles on Jesus
Christ and the Holy Spirit present the antitrinitarian view
that only the Father is God. Obviously, in spite of the foreword's claim to the contrary, it was to present this doctrinal slant that the Watchtower Society produced its own
Bible dictionary in the first place, rather than utilize those
already available through bookstores.

Aid to Bible Understanding was replaced in 1988 by
the two-volume *Insight on the Scriptures.*

Listening to the Great Teacher, 1971

During the period from May 1970 through August 1971
The Watchtower magazine featured brief articles about Jesus
for parents to read with young children. Then in the summer of 1971 these articles were adapted, along with other

material, to form this pocket-size book of forty-six short chapters. Besides teaching simple moral lessons on forgiveness, obedience, truthfulness, and the importance of saying thank you, the book also shows Jesus nailed to an upright stake instead of a cross and says about him: "Jesus always did what was right. He did not pretend to be someone that he really was not. He did not tell people that he was God" (p. 26). Of the millions of copies distributed, many were purchased by unsuspecting non-Witness parents who had no idea that this children's book would implant Jehovah's Witness doctrine in their youngsters' minds.

"The Nations Shall Know That I Am Jehovah"—How? 1971

A commentary on selected portions of the Book of Ezekiel, this volume covers Ezekiel from beginning to end but omits discussion of chapters 5, 12–20, 22, 25–32, 35, 41, 42, and 44–46. It presents much of Ezekiel's prophetic writing as having two fulfillments: an original fulfillment upon ancient Israel, and a modern fulfillment upon Jehovah's Witnesses. Thus the valley of dry bones in Ezekiel, chapter 37, is said to picture the condition of those associated with the Watchtower organization during a period of relative inactivity toward the end of World War I, before God "resurrected them to vigorous public activity again in preaching" in the spring of 1919 (p. 342). But prophecies directed against Jerusalem are interpreted as foretelling "Christendom's fiery destruction" (p. 212).

One of the unique Watchtower teachings highlighted in *"The Nations Shall Know That I Am Jehovah"—How?* is the belief that the name Jehovah is "the one name to call upon for salvation" (p. 333) and that use of that name for God is a key identifying mark of the true religion.

Theocratic Ministry School Guidebook, 1971

This replaced the book *Qualified to Be Ministers* (1967 revision) and is, essentially, a streamlined version of the same.

New World Translation of the Holy Scriptures (revised), 1971
Please see the discussion of the 1961 edition in this chapter.

The Bible in Living English, by Steven T. Byington, 1972
Unique among modern publications of the Watchtower Society, this Bible is the first and only volume since 1942 to carry the writer's byline, and, even more amazingly, the byline of a non-Jehovah's Witness. In an appendix to *The Bible in Living English* titled "The Translator," it is stated that "Mr. Byington regularly attended a Congregational church that later merged with another church to form the United Church of Ballard Vale, Massachusetts" (p. 1597).

While I was a Jehovah's Witness during the 1970s I had occasion to meet an elderly woman then living in Brockton, Massachusetts, who formerly attended the same Congregational church as Steven T. Byington. She remembered him as "a maverick who took it upon himself to interrupt the minister during Sunday morning sermons, standing up in his pew and contradicting whatever the pastor had just said."

Concerning the translator, the *Awake!* magazine of October 22, 1972, said, "Byington, who died in 1957, was not one of Jehovah's witnesses. Yet he had a keen desire faithfully to render the Bible in easy-to-read English" (pp. 20–21). *The Watchtower* of October 1, 1972, was a bit more straightforward about the aspect of the translation that led to its publication by Jehovah's Witnesses, referring to it as "a new translation by Steven T. Byington, in which the Hebrew Tetragrammaton is consistently rendered as 'Jehovah'" (p. 606). In the appendix on Byington the Watchtower Society comments that he "appreciated the importance of incorporating the divine name 'Jehovah' in his work, especially since its omission from other translations definitely obscured certain texts" (p. 1597).

This appendix goes on to say about Byington that he was born in 1868 and decided before the age of thirteen to translate the Bible into modern English. To that end, after graduating from the University of Vermont, he did one year of postgraduate study at Union Theological Seminary and a half year at Oberlin Theological Seminary, continuing after that to study biblical languages privately while working a secular job. The actual translation of *The Bible in Living English* took more than forty years; Byington commenced it in 1898 at the age of thirty and translated a few verses at a time during spare minutes until he retired from his secular job in 1940 at the age of seventy-two. He completed the work in 1943, but was unable to find a publisher. The appendix states that it was "after his death in 1957" that the Watchtower organization "received the publication rights for the entire work," presumably through some financial arrangement with Byington's heirs.

It was evidently never the intention of the Watchtower Society that this Bible should come into everyday usage among Jehovah's Witnesses. (One hundred thousand copies were printed in 1972 and fifty thousand in 1973, compared with a first-edition printing of 1 million copies for the Society's own New World Translation in 1961, and a total printing of more than 23 million for the New World Translation by the time *The Bible in Living English* was released.) After all, despite Steven T. Byington's unorthodox Sunday morning manners in church and his fellowship with a liberal denomination, his translation is essentially orthodox. He has John 1:1 say, "the Word was God" rather than "the Word was a god," and he has Matthew 24:3 refer to Christ's "coming," rather than "presence" as in the New World Translation, which renders these verses to conform to Watchtower doctrine. So, Jehovah's Witnesses would find it embarrassing to use this version in their door-to-door preaching or as a regular pulpit Bible. Rather, the Watchtower Society apparently felt it was worthwhile to have in print another independent translation prominently featuring the name *Jehovah.*

Still, the discerning reader will note that *The Bible in Living English* uses this rendering of the divine name only in the Old Testament where the Tetragrammaton actually appears in ancient Hebrew manuscripts. It does not follow the example of the New World Translation, which takes the liberty of inserting the name *Jehovah* throughout the New Testament despite the Watchtower Society's own admission that "no early surviving Greek manuscript of the 'New Testament' contains the personal name of God" (*The Watchtower,* March 1, 1991, p. 28).

Moreover, the terms under which Jehovah's Witnesses gained the rights to *The Bible in Living English* apparently included the stipulation that it be "printed as its translator, Steven T. Byington, prepared it . . . according to his typewritten manuscript" (title page).

So, the translator's preface still contains an admission that the Watchtower Society would hardly have published under other circumstances, namely, that "as to the Old Testament name of God, certainly the spelling and pronunciation 'Jehovah' were originally a blunder" (p. 7).

Organization for Kingdom-Preaching and Disciple-Making, 1972

This organizational manual and catechism replaced the 1967 book "*Your Word Is a Lamp to My Foot.*" It caused considerable internal turmoil by calling for the appointment of a body of elders in each congregation, with the chief responsible positions to rotate annually among these elders. This in effect unseated the powerful "congregation servant" (pastor) in each local JW church—some of whom had ruled unchallenged for many years—and made him just one of the elders. The rotation arrangement was gradually phased out after a dozen years, with one position at a time being made permanent once again.

This book was replaced in 1983 by *Organized to Accomplish Our Ministry.*

Paradise Restored to Mankind—By Theocracy! 1972

Jehovah's Witnesses are identified as "A Modern-Day Haggai" (p. 49) in this commentary on the books of Haggai and Zechariah. And both Hebrew prophets are presented as prophesying about events related to the Watchtower organization's activities from the year 1914 onward. Thus the inspired prediction of Zechariah 2:11 that "many nations will certainly become joined to Jehovah in that day" (NWT) is said to have had its fulfillment "from 1935 C.E. onward, four years after the anointed remnant had embraced the designation, Jehovah's witnesses" (p. 173).

Oddly enough, after admitting that several of the organization's prophecies "proved to be incorrect in the light of historic events" (p. 352) the discussion goes on to applaud "the disfellowshiping or excommunicating of religious apostates or rebels from the theocratic organization" because these individuals are "false prophets" (pp. 354–355). And it declares this in connection with such renegade JWs:

> Jehovah, the God of the true prophets, will put all false prophets to shame either by not fulfilling the false prediction of such self-assuming prophets or by having His own prophecies fulfilled in a way opposite to that predicted by the false prophets. (pp. 353–354)

Comprehensive Concordance of the New World Translation of the Holy Scriptures, 1973

Ever since the release of the first portion of the *New World Translation* in 1950, Jehovah's Witnesses have encountered difficulty with the use of popular concordances. This, of course, is because of the unique renderings in their Bible. For example, such words as *cross* and *crucify* do not appear in connection with Christ's death, but are replaced by *torture stake* and *impale*. And the name

Jehovah appears thousands of times in the Old Testament and hundreds of times in the New Testament.

Just as it proves useful to the Witnesses themselves, this concordance can also prove helpful to Christians interested in locating some of the New World Translation's unusual renderings, such as *active force* used in place of *Spirit* at Genesis 1:2.

God's Kingdom of a Thousand Years Has Approached, 1973

The very title of this book stirred excitement among Jehovah's Witnesses when it was released just prior to 1975. Since the mid-1960s the organization had been building up the expectation that Armageddon would put an end to this world and usher in God's kingdom by the fall of 1975. "WHY ARE YOU LOOKING FORWARD TO 1975?" is the bold title of a major *Watchtower* study article that appeared in 1968 (August 15 issue, p. 494). After presenting a few pages of argumentation, the article sums up a main point this way:

> Are we to assume from this study that the battle of Armageddon will be all over by the autumn of 1975, and the long-looked-for thousand-year reign of Christ will begin by then? . . . It may involve only a difference of weeks or months, not years. (*The Watchtower*, August 15, 1968, p. 499)

So, it was with these high expectations that Jehovah's Witnesses in 1973 received their new book *God's Kingdom of a Thousand Years Has Approached*. And the book did not disappoint them.

Ironically, it begins its chronological discussions with a brief history of other attempts to predict the start of Christ's reign. It tells of "a Lutheran theologian named Johann Albrecht Bengel" (1687–1752) of Wuerttemberg, Germany, who pointed to "the beginning of the millennium at the year 1836" (p. 184). Then it refers to William Miller

(1781–1849) who "taught that the world was coming to an end in 1843" (p. 185). Next it passes on to Watchtower founder Charles Taze Russell and acknowledges this in his writings:

> The year 1874 was calculated as being the end of six millenniums of sin among mankind. From this latter date mankind was understood to be in the seventh millennium. (p. 187)

The book now explains that Russell made an error in his calculations "by inserting 100 years into the Bible chronology during the period of the Judges" (p. 208), and that correcting this error moves forward "the end of six thousand years of man's existence into the decade of the 1970s" (p. 209). The logical conclusion, of course, is that the millennial reign of Christ can be expected to begin in the mid-1970s.

Also of interest is the fact that *God's Kingdom of a Thousand Years Has Approached* provides misleading information as to when the Watchtower Society revised its teaching on the date of Christ's invisible presence. It says:

> In the year 1943 the Watch Tower Bible and Tract Society published the book *"The Truth Shall Make You Free."* In its chapter 11, entitled "The Count of Time," it did away with the insertion of 100 years into the period of the Judges. . . . Naturally, this did away with the year 1874 C.E. as the date of return of the Lord Jesus Christ and the beginning of his invisible presence or parousia. (*God's Kingdom of a Thousand Years Has Approached,* pp. 209–210)

But 1943 was not the first time that the Society replaced 1874 with 1914 as the start of Christ's presence. Thirteen years earlier, in 1930, its *Golden Age* magazine said:

> In Matthew 24, Jesus gives His disciples some proofs that He would be present. . . . These tangible evidences will be the beginning of the work of destroying the present evil conditions and systems. This work of destruction began in 1914. . . . If it is true that Jesus has been present since the year 1914, then it

must be admitted that nobody has seen Him with his natural eyes. (*Golden Age,* 1930, p. 503)

Why does the Watchtower Society incorrectly cite its own literature, indicating that the change was first made in the 1943 book instead of referring to the 1930 magazine? It may simply be an oversight. But some have theorized that the change was made in 1930 under pressure of necessity, forced by the failure of prophecies based on the old chronology, although a new chronological basis for the change was not provided until 1943—thus making the unsupported assertion 1930 an embarrassment the Society would prefer to forget.[4]

True Peace and Security—From What Source? 1973

Release of this book shortly before 1975 served to heighten the expectations of Jehovah's Witnesses for the end of the world in that year. The title itself helped accomplish this, since the expression "peace and security" is understood among JWs as a final signal that the end is at hand:

> There is yet one more definite event to come that serves as an *unmistakable signal* that world destruction is imminent. This signal was pointed to by the apostle Paul when he wrote: "Jehovah's day is coming exactly as a thief in the night. Whenever it is that they are saying: 'Peace and security!' then sudden destruction is to be instantly upon them." (p. 89, emphasis theirs)

The remainder of the book uses strong language to push people into joining the Watchtower organization as the only way to survive imminent world destruction. These chapter headings exemplify the tone of the discussion: "The Choice We All Face" (ch. 1), "World Destruction First—Then World Peace" (ch. 4), "When Will the Foretold World Destruction Come?" (ch. 7), "Who Will the Survivors Be?" (ch. 8), and "Survivors Must Be 'No Part of the World'" (ch. 11).

A revised edition of this book with full-color illustrations was published in 1986 under the title *True Peace and Security—How Can You Find It?* Please see the discussion in our next chapter.

God's "Eternal Purpose" Now Triumphing for Man's Good, 1974

Without actually mentioning the year 1975 this book continues to stir up the expectations raised for that date in prior Watchtower publications. It states that "the seventh creative 'day' began, about six thousand years ago," and that "during the thousand years that the Great Serpent and his demon 'seed' are abyssed, Jehovah God will reverse all the wickedness. . . . By means of the thousand-year reign of his Son Jesus Christ" (p. 189), and that "God's 'eternal purpose'" is that the "seventh creative 'day' will end up blessed" (p. 190). Elsewhere the book indicates that this "seventh creative 'day'" is 7000 years long, and that its second half of 3,500 years "begins, 526 B.C.E." (p. 131). Simple arithmetic indicates that it will end in A.D. 2975, with the thousand-year reign of Christ also ending then and therefore starting in 1975. Witnesses who did the mathematical calculations saw this as a very specific prophecy of the end in 1975.

Is This Life All There Is? 1974

Simply, clearly, and persuasively this book presents the Watchtower Society's teaching on death and the condition of the dead. It argues that "the human soul is the entire man" (p. 41) and therefore does not live on after death. The spirit "is only a life-force that has no conscious existence apart from a body" (p. 51). So, according to Jehovah's Witnesses, man at death ceases to exist. No part of man survives death. The wicked receive no punishment after death. And even the righteous have no continuity of existence but are "re-created" in the resurrection from a pattern kept in God's memory (p. 172). For a refutation of these teachings and their biblical arguments, please see my book *Jehovah's Witnesses Answered Verse by Verse* (Baker Book House, 1986).

Christians may wish to give Jehovah's Witnesses a piece of their own advice by referring them to these words on page 46 of *Is This Life All There Is?*:

> God, who is himself "the God of truth" and who hates lies, will not look with favor on persons who cling to organizations that teach falsehood. . . . And, really, would you want to be even associated with a religion that had not been honest with you?

Is This Life All There Is? was written by Watchtower headquarters staff member Reinhard Lengtat, according to former Governing Body member Raymond Franz in his book *Crisis of Conscience* (Commentary Press, 1983, p. 228).

A separate booklet of study questions allows *Is This Life All There Is?* to be studied at congregation meetings and in private with individuals.

1975 Yearbook of Jehovah's Witnesses, 1974

Although annual yearbooks have been produced throughout most of this century and feature histories of the Witnesses' activities in various countries as well as Bible verses and discussions for daily devotions during the designated year, only those yearbooks of special significance are listed and discussed here. The *1975 Yearbook* is of interest because it contains a 223-page history of Jehovah's Witnesses in the United States.

While the discussions of the sect's activities in foreign countries found in the *Yearbooks* of other years consist largely of anecdotes about missionaries and how they won over local people, the *1975 Yearbook's* story of the sect in the United States naturally deals with its origin and its organizational development over the years. Although the account is totally one-sided as a propaganda piece for

"God's organization" there is much of value to learn from it, especially when other versions of the same events are available for comparison and contrast.

This *Yearbook* provides enough information, for example, to establish that the Watch Tower movement began not as a divine creation raised up by God to restore true Christianity but rather as a schismatic faction that broke away from a Second Adventist splinter group in 1879, when Charles Taze Russell resigned as an assistant editor of the Adventist magazine *The Herald of the Morning* and began publishing his own magazine *Zion's Watch Tower and Herald of Christ's Presence.* (See chapter 1.)

Although surrounded with sugarcoated explanations, an admission is also found here that Watchtower followers had expected that in the year 1925 "the remnant of Christ's anointed followers would go to heaven to be part of the Kingdom and that the faithful men of old, such as Abraham, David and others, would be resurrected as princes to take over the government of the earth as part of God's Kingdom" (p. 146, quoting Governing Body member Albert D. Schroeder).

The *Yearbook* account tries to pass off the failed expectations as originating with the readers rather than with the writers of Watchtower literature. It quotes an unidentified "Anna MacDonald" as saying, concerning "many brothers," that "instead of its being considered a 'probability,' they read into it that it was a 'certainty'" (p. 146). But an examination of what the Watchtower Society actually published in 1920 reveals that the expectations for 1925 did not have to be "read into" the material, because they were spelled out in black and white: "Therefore we may confidently expect that 1925 will mark the return of Abraham, Isaac, Jacob and the faithful prophets of old" (*Millions Now Living Will Never Die,* 1920, pp. 89–90; see discussion for additional details).

Released toward the end of 1974, the *1975 Yearbook* continues to raise expectations for the autumn of 1975. Referring to the book *Life Everlasting—in Freedom of the Sons of God* released in 1966, the *Yearbook* offers these comments:

> The chronological chart . . . identified 1975 as the "end of 6th 1,000-year day of man's existence (in early autumn)." This certainly raised questions. Does this mean that Babylon the Great will go down by 1975? Will Armageddon be over, with Satan bound, by then? "It could," acknowledged F. W. Franz, the Watch Tower Society's vice-president, after posing similar questions at the "God's Sons of Liberty" District Assembly in Baltimore, Maryland. However, he added, in essence: "But we are not saying. All things are possible with God. But we are not saying. And don't any of you be specific in saying anything that is going to happen between now and 1975. But the big point of it all is this, dear friends: Time is short. Time is running out, no question about that." (p. 256)

Also of interest are the pictures inside the front and back covers showing some of the Watchtower's multi-million-dollar real estate holdings, as well as panoramic photographs of Yankee Stadium and the Polo Grounds packed with more than one-quarter million people in 1958, the last time Jehovah's Witnesses worldwide tried to assemble for their annual convention in a single city.

Man's Salvation out of World Distress at Hand, 1975

Released just weeks before the anticipated end of the world in the autumn of 1975, this book proved somewhat disappointing to Jehovah's Witnesses. Although many expected a brief, concise tool for last-minute evangelizing, instead they received a wordy 384-page slow-moving text—at least a year's worth of material for group study at congregation meetings. Among other things, it tediously examines messianic prophecies of Isaiah and end-times prophecies from elsewhere in the Bible without making any specific application to the 1970s.

As if anticipating that it would be studied after the 1975 prophecies would fail, the chapter titled "Awaiting the 'New Heavens and a New Earth'" devotes several pages (284–301) to the problem of impatience and to answering ridiculers whose aim is "to cast doubt upon Bible prophecy or to unsettle the faith and conviction of Jehovah's Christian witnesses" (p. 289).

Good News—To Make You Happy, 1976

Although initially released in English, this pocket-size book is "designed particularly to be used in bringing the Bible's message to Orientals and others who may have had little or no previous acquaintance with the Bible's teachings," according to *Awake!* magazine (October 22, 1976, p. 22). Many Oriental faces and settings are featured in the illustrations, and the message is confined to introductory and basic Watchtower teachings.

Holy Spirit—The Force Behind the Coming New Order, 1976

Even before its cover is opened, this book proclaims the Watchtower Society's teaching that the Holy Spirit is "a force, not a person" (p. 12), "the impersonal active force of God" (p. 14), "an invisible active force by means of which he gets his will done" (p. 11). To a certain extent this concept is similar to that found in the 1977 motion picture *Star Wars,* which has Luke Skywalker and his friends greet one another with the expression, "May the Force be with you!"

Watchtower writers here go through the Old and New Testaments discussing passages about the Holy Spirit and interpreting them to harmonize with this teaching. (For refutation, please see my book *Jehovah's Witnesses Answered Verse by Verse,* Baker Book House, 1986.) Notably missing from the text is any comment on the expressions found in

Acts 5:3–4 and 2 Corinthians 3:17–18, which identify the Holy Spirit as God.

Your Youth—Getting the Best out of It, 1976

Targeted primarily at teenagers in Jehovah's Witness congregations, this book discusses such subjects as drugs, alcohol, sports, entertainment, schooling, masturbation, homosexuality, dating, and courtship. It interprets Bible verses to teach the youngsters the Watchtower Society's view on each subject.

This book was replaced in 1989 by *Questions Young People Ask: Answers That Work.*

Life Does Have a Purpose, 1977

People who "doubt the existence of a Creator" or "view him as a cold, remote Being—unconcerned about mankind" are the intended audience for this book (*Our Kingdom Service,* October 1977, p. 4). It presents arguments calculated to lead such skeptics into belief in God and into further study with Jehovah's Witnesses.

Life Does Have a Purpose was written by Ed Dunlap, who was later convicted of apostasy by a Watchtower judicial committee and expelled in 1980, according to former Governing Body member Raymond Franz in his book *Crisis of Conscience,* p. 228.

Our Incoming World Government—God's Kingdom, 1977

Although not set up as a verse-by-verse commentary, this volume actually comments in detail on much of chapters 2, 4, 7, and 12 of the Book of Daniel. It does this in the course of tracing the succession of world powers in Bible history and the Watchtower Society's interpretation of end-times prophecies.

Our Incoming World Government—God's Kingdom continues the tradition of egocentrically interpreting prophecy in Scripture as applying specifically to the Watchtower Society. Thus the "time, times, and half a time" of Daniel 12:7 is said to have begun on December 28, 1914 and ended on June 21, 1918:

> On that day the American federal court sentenced the president and the secretary-treasurer of the Watch Tower Bible and Tract Society and five of their headquarters associates to long prison terms, amounting to a total of 140 years. (p. 128)

Similarly, the "1290 days" of Daniel 12:11 ran from "the peace conference that assembled in Versailles, France, on January 18, 1919 . . . when the eight representatives of the Watch Tower Bible and Tract Society were still under restraint in the Atlanta federal penitentiary" (pp. 136–137), and ended at "sundown, September 9, 1922," in the midst of a Watchtower convention at which J. F. Rutherford presented a resolution that challenged world rulers and a speech that exhorted those attending to "advertise, advertise, advertise, the King and his kingdom" (pp. 137–138). Moreover, the "1335 days" of Daniel 12:12 began the day after that convention, September 14, 1922, and ended on May 19, 1926, midway between May conventions in Magdeburg, Germany, where Rutherford delivered the talk "Comfort for the People" and London, England, where Rutherford's words "proved to be the start of the pouring out of the fifth 'plague' as foretold in Revelation 16:10, 11" (pp. 140–142).

Another point found in *Our Incoming World Government—God's Kingdom* that is potentially useful in reasoning with Jehovah's Witnesses is its discussion of Jesus' words regarding a "faithful and discreet slave" in Matthew 24:45–47 (NWT). The Watchtower Society's literature had taught for a number of years that this refers to a single individual, namely, Charles Taze Russell: "THE WATCH TOWER unhesitatingly proclaims brother Russell as 'that faithful and wise servant'" (*The Watch Tower*, March 1, 1917, p. 6049 [Society's reprints]).

Today the Society teaches a collective "servant" made up of the body of Christ, or the "anointed class." But, *Our Incoming World Government—God's Kingdom* admits that Jesus gave the parable to encourage each of his followers individually to be a faithful and discreet slave rather than an evil slave. He was not pointing to either Charles Taze Russell or a slave class:

> The King Jesus Christ detests lukewarm service, halfhearted attention. He wants no hypocrites in his kingdom.
> This vital point is emphasized by Jesus Christ in the illustrations of the "faithful and discreet slave" and "that evil slave," the illustrations that he gave right after urging his disciples to "prove themselves ready" at *all* times. (Matt. 24:45–51) There is a grand reward reserved for Christ's disciples who prove themselves to be faithful, discreet and loving slaves of his, uncompromisingly devoted to his handling of the promised world government. (pp. 158–159)

This interpretation nullifies the Watchtower Society's claim to authority, namely, that it is to be obeyed as the mouthpiece of an elite faithful and discreet slave class.

Shining as Illuminators in the World, 1977

This served as the textbook for a two-week Pioneer Service School attended by full-time door-to-door workers, beginning in December 1977.

Booklets

Watchtower booklets, almost too numerous to mention, are simply listed here. Only those of lasting significance are discussed. Most are simply printed transcripts of talks given at major conventions.

"Children" Study Questions, 1942

Designed to be used with the book *Children,* this booklet presents questions on each paragraph. In this way the book could be studied systematically, paragraph by paragraph. Similar booklets accompany other Watchtower study books to facilitate their use in home studies and/or congregation meetings. Eventually, Watchtower books began to be printed with the questions at the bottom of each page instead of in a separate booklet.

Hope, 1942

Jehovah's Witnesses: Who Are They? What Is Their Work? 1942

Organization Instructions, 1942

This booklet outlining procedures for meetings and field ministry was originally issued only to congregation overseers and full-time pioneer field workers. In 1945 a revised and expanded edition was issued to active Jehovah's Witnesses in general. An eight-page insert of additional amendments was issued in October, 1946. In 1949 this was replaced by a booklet titled *Counsel on Theocratic Organization for Jehovah's Witnesses*.

Peace—Can It Last? 1942

"The New World" Study Questions, 1942

See *"Children" Study Questions,* 1942

Course in Theocratic Ministry, 1943

Perhaps the most significant organizational change introduced by new Watchtower president Nathan Knorr was the creation of a ministry school in each local Jehovah's Witness congregation. *Course in Theocratic Ministry* was the training program's first textbook. This 96-page booklet features fifty-two lessons as well as instructions on how to operate the school. In the form of a new hour-long congregation meeting, the school provided speech training for several members each week while the rest of the congregation listened.

The immediate result was that, within a year of the school's creation, the organization began to phase out the use of portable phonographs in its house-to-house ministry. Instead of playing records of J. F. Rutherford's lectures on people's doorsteps, Jehovah's Witnesses began speaking themselves, delivering oral sermons to each householder who would listen.

Then, in 1945, the Watchtower Society began using the best speakers in each congregation to deliver public lectures based on outlines supplied by Brooklyn headquarters. Congregation members would distribute handbills from door to door and carry placards in downtown business districts inviting interested persons from the general public to attend these lectures. The membership would also attend to provide a full audience and to initiate one-on-one assistance for newcomers who were viewed as potential converts.

The overall training program produced dramatic growth in the Witness organization. The number of individuals preaching from house to house doubled in five years, from 126,000 in 1943 to 261,000 in 1948, and quadrupled in ten years to 520,000 in 1953.

Other textbooks for the course included *Theocratic Aid to Kingdom Publishers* (1945) and *"Equipped for Every Good Work"* (1946).

Fighting for Liberty on the Home Front, 1943

Freedom in the New World, 1943

Freedom of Worship, 1943

"The Truth Shall Make You Free" Study Questions, 1943
    See *"Children" Study Questions,* 1942.

One World, One Government, 1944

Religion Reaps the Whirlwind, 1944

The Coming World Regeneration, 1944

"The Kingdom Is at Hand" Study Questions, 1944
  See *"Children" Study Questions,* 1942.

"The Kingdom of God Is Nigh," 1944

"The Commander to the Peoples," 1945

"The Meek Inherit the Earth," 1945

"Be Glad, Ye Nations," 1946

"The Prince of Peace," 1946

The Joy of All the People, 1947

The Permanent Governor of All Nations, 1948

The Watchtower Story, 1948

Counsel On Theocratic Organization for Jehovah's Witnesses, 1949

Restricted in its circulation, this organization manual supplanted the *Organization Instructions* booklet (1942). It was given only to baptized Jehovah's Witnesses. The "company servant" (pastor) of each JW "company" (congregation) was instructed to write the name and address of the Witness issued the booklet in a space provided for that purpose on page 2.

Subjects covered include positions of responsibility in the local congregation, how to conduct the various meetings, and how to conduct and report witnessing activity. The sales-oriented nature of the organization is revealed in these instructions regarding literature sales and man hours in the door-to-door work:

> The company chart, provided by the Society and placed at the front of the Kingdom Hall, will serve a useful purpose in the service meeting. Quotas on the chart should be taken seriously, and counsel offered by servants as to how these can be met. A company should strive to reach its quotas at the beginning of the service year and maintain them throughout. (pp. 42–43)

The Kingdom Hope of All Mankind, 1949

Can You Live Forever in Happiness on Earth? 1950

Defending and Legally Establishing the Good News, 1950

This ninety-six-page booklet consists mainly of legal precedents in federal, state, and local courts upholding the right of Jehovah's Witnesses to sell literature in public places and from house to house, to call at homes uninvited, to enter multiunit apartment buildings, to carry on their activities without police permits, and so on. Witnesses would carry the booklet with them and show it to property owners or policemen who challenged their activities.

Evolution Versus the New World, 1950

Will Religion Meet the World Crisis? 1951

Dwelling Together in Unity, 1952

Excerpts From Selective Service Regulations, 1952

God's Way Is Love, 1952

After Armageddon—God's New World, 1953

Basis for Belief in a New World, 1953

"Preach the Word," 1953

This booklet features one-page printed introductions to the Watchtower message in dozens of languages, including those with unique alphabets such as Arabic, Urdu, and Chinese. Thus equipped, a Jehovah's Witness is prepared to encounter non-English-speaking people in his door-to-door activity.

"Preach the Word" was replaced in 1983 by *Good News for All Nations.*

Working Together in Unity, 1953

Counsel to Watch Tower Missionaries, 1954

"This Good News of the Kingdom," 1954

Unassigned Territory in the United States, 1954

Christendom or Christianity—Which One Is "the Light of the World"? 1955

Preaching Together in Unity, 1955
  This is an updated organizational manual. Please see *Counsel on Theocratic Organization for Jehovah's Witnesses* above.

What Do the Scriptures Say About "Survival After Death"? 1955

World Conquest Soon—By God's Kingdom, 1955

Manual of Theocratic News Service Information, 1956

Healing of the Nations Has Drawn Near, 1957

God's Kingdom Rules—Is the World's End Near? 1958

"Look! I Am Making All Things New," 1959

Preaching and Teaching in Peace and Unity, 1960
  This is an updated organizational manual. Please see *Counsel on Theocratic Organization for Jehovah's Witnesses* above. This 1960 booklet was replaced in 1967 by the hardcover book *"Your Word Is a Lamp to My Foot."*

Security During "War of the Great Day of God the Almighty," 1960

Blood, Medicine and the Law of God, 1961

Sermon Outlines, 1961
  Listing main points and Scripture references under numerous topics, this booklet enabled a Witness to speak on subjects brought up for discussion by potential converts. It was replaced by *Bible Topics for Discussion* in 1977.

Watch Tower Publications Index (1961), 1961

When All Nations Unite Under God's Kingdom, 1961

Take Courage—God's Kingdom Is at Hand! 1962

"The Word"—Who Is He? According to John, 1962

Living in Hope of a Righteous New World, 1963

When God is King Over All the Earth, 1963

Report on "Everlasting Good News" Assembly of Jehovah's Witnesses, 1963

Between 1904 and 1969 dozens of souvenir convention reports were published in connection with the sect's large gatherings, but only those of 1905 and 1963 are listed here. Filled with artists' drawings and photographs of ordinary members and Watchtower dignitaries, the convention reports advertised new books released at these assemblies, documented their international flavor, and reported on the programs presented.

"Peace Among Men of Good Will" or Armageddon—Which? 1964

Questions on the Book "Babylon the Great Has Fallen!" God's Kingdom Rules! 1964

"This Good News of the Kingdom" (revised), 1965

World Government on the Shoulder of the Prince of Peace, 1965

What Has God's Kingdom Been Doing Since 1914? 1966

Jehovah's Witnesses, 1966

Rescuing a Great Crowd of Mankind out of Armageddon, 1967

Learn to Read And Write, 1967

This booklet is a tool for reaching illiterate individuals with the Watchtower's message. It begins with pictorial lessons on the letters of the alphabet, progresses to simple doctrinal lessons in large print, and concludes with small-print lessons on Armageddon and "The Theocratic Organization"—all in 64 pages.

Man's Rule About to Give Way to God's Rule, 1968

Questions on the Book "Then Is Finished the Mystery of God," 1969

Study Questions for the Book "Is the Bible Really the Word of God?" 1969

The Approaching Peace of a Thousand Years, 1969

Saving the Human Race—In the Kingdom Way, 1970

Convention Organization, 1971

When All Nations Collide, Head On, With God, 1971

Divine Rulership—The Only Hope of All Mankind, 1972

Divine Victory—Its Meaning for Distressed Humanity, 1973

Human Plans Failing as God's Purpose Succeeds, 1974

A Secure Future—How You Can Find It, 1975

Is There a God Who Cares? 1975

One World, One Government, Under God's Sovereignty, 1975

There Is Much More to Life! 1975

Bible Topics for Discussion, 1977
     This replaced *Sermon Outlines* (1961) as a quick-reference tool for answering doctrinal questions.

Jehovah's Witnesses and the Question of Blood, 1977

"Pay Attention to Yourselves and to All the Flock" (first booklet), 1977

This served as the textbook in a Kingdom Ministry School training course for congregation elders. Circulation of the booklet was limited to the elders themselves.

Tracts and Pamphlets

Watchtower tracts and pamphlets are almost too numerous to mention. They are simply listed here. Only those of lasting significance are discussed.

Kingdom News No. 10 (Life in the New Earth Under New Heavens), 1942

Kingdom News No. 11 (The People Have a Right to Good News Now), 1942

Kingdom News No. 12 (The Last War Wins Peace Eternal), 1943

Kingdom News No. 13 (Education for Life in the New World), 1944

Kingdom News No. 14 (Overcoming Fear of What Is Coming on the Earth), 1944

Kingdom News No. 15 (World Conspiracy Against the Truth), 1946

Quebec's Burning Hate for God and Christ and Freedom Is the Shame of All Canada, 1946

Quebec. You Have Failed Your People! 1946

Awake from Sleep! 1951

Hell-Fire—Bible Truth or Pagan Scare? 1951

Jehovah's Witnesses. Communists or Christians? 1951

What Do Jehovah's Witnesses Believe? 1951

Hope for the Dead, 1952

How Valuable Is the Bible? 1952

Life in a New World, 1952

The Trinity. Divine Mystery or Pagan Myth? 1952

Do You Believe in Evolution or the Bible? 1953

Man's Only Hope for Peace, 1953

The Sign of Christ's Presence, 1953

Which Is the Right Religion? 1953

How Has Christendom Failed All Mankind? 1958

Would You Like to Understand the Bible? 1968

Kingdom News No. 16 (Is Time Running Out for Mankind?), 1973

I recall being present at the summer 1973 "Divine Victory" International Assembly of Jehovah's Witnesses when a packet of these tracts was provided for everyone in the audience. They were to be distributed door-to-door worldwide during a ten-day period, from September 21 through 30. I remember President Knorr telling us that breaking a leg would be about the only thing that might excuse us from participation in this vital work. The world's end was close, and it was essential that every household receive a copy as their official notification of this fact. The *1975 Yearbook* reports that 512,738 people took part in distributing 43,320,048 copies in the United States during September (p. 252).

Kingdom News No. 17 (Has Religion Betrayed God and Man?), 1973

Kingdom News No. 18 (Government by God. Are You For It—Or Against It?), 1974

Kingdom News No. 19 (Is This All There Is to Life?), 1974

Kingdom News No. 20 (Would You Welcome Some Good News?), 1975

Kingdom News No. 22 (How Crime and Violence Will Be Stopped), 1976

Kingdom News No. 23 (Why So Much Suffering—If God Cares?), 1976

Blood Transfusion—Why Not for Jehovah's Witnesses, 1977

Kingdom News No. 24 (The Family—Can It Survive?), 1977

6

The Frederick W. Franz Era
1977–1992

President
Born September 12, 1893
Died December 22, 1992

Periodicals

The Watchtower Announcing Jehovah's Kingdom

This 32-page semimonthly magazine remains the Watchtower Society's chief means of instructing members in doctrine and practice. It is also the principal publication used in proselytizing. As of this writing *The Watchtower* is published in 112 languages with a total of 16,400,000 copies per issue.

Well over one hundred *Watchtower* magazine quotations tracing doctrinal changes through the Franz era are included in my book *Index of Watchtower Errors* (Baker Book House, 1990). Continually changing teachings are monitored through the quarterly Christian publication *Comments from the Friends,* P.O. Box 840, Stoughton, MA 02072.

Bound volumes of *The Watchtower* produced shortly after the end of each calendar year normally contain faithful reproductions of the individual magazines (with blank space replacing back page advertisements for other publications). There are, however, some notable exceptions during the Franz era. For example, the front cover of the September 15, 1982, *Watchtower* displayed a red sunset silhouetting a building with an elevated porch—trimmed down a bit from a picture that had appeared earlier as a Johnnie Walker Red scotch whisky ad in several popular magazines. After the liquor company's lawyer contacted Watchtower headquarters, the Society agreed to stop using the copyrighted drawing on its cover. So, when the 1982 bound volume was printed, the cover of the September 15th issue featured a different picture—a landscape showing trees with mountains in the background, predominantly blue instead of red. Foreign language editions printed after the U.S. English edition also carried the new cover.

Similarly, page 13 of the original June 1, 1989, *Watchtower* displayed a photograph of a married couple over the heading, "God's Word says, 'Let marriage be honorable.'" In the bound volume reprint a different couple's photograph is substituted without explanation.

But perhaps the most interesting change is that found on page 12 of the January 1, 1989, *Watchtower*. In the original magazine, paragraph 8 ends with the statement that the apostle Paul's missionary activity laid the foundation for "a work that would be completed in our 20th century"— a subtle prophecy that "the end" will come by 1999. This sentence is changed without fanfare in the bound volume reprint to read "a work that would be completed in our day," thus eliminating the prophetic deadline.

Some have compared such alterations with those described in George Orwell's novel *Nineteen Eighty-Four* (Signet Classic edition, pages 36–37). In Orwell's futuristic, totalitarian state where "Big Brother is watching you!" books and periodicals are systematically rewritten to con-

ceal mistaken prophecies and thus make Big Brother's ruling party appear always to have been correct.

Awake!

Offered from door to door along with *The Watchtower,*
this magazine serves to draw the interest of nonreligious
people with articles on nonbiblical subjects.

Our Kingdom Service, renamed Our Kingdom Ministry in 1982

This members-only monthly publication features
instructions for carrying on the house-to-house ministry,
as well as news about the organization's conventions and
new publications.

The word *ministry* appeared in the title for twenty
years because the leadership taught that all Jehovah's Witnesses were ministers. In 1976 this teaching was reversed,
and the word *ministry* removed. In 1982 the teaching was
reversed again—back to the previous point of view—and
the word *ministry* put back in.

Books

Making Your Family Life Happy, 1978

For the most part this book consists of the same sound
advice that a Christian counselor or psychologist would
give on family matters. It was produced to aid Jehovah's
Witnesses in this area and also to serve, like the *Awake!*
magazine, as a tool for drawing the interest of nonreligious
people.

My Book of Bible Stories, 1978

At first glance this book of familiar Bible stories looks
much like others available at secular and Christian bookstores: large print and simple text on big pages, with many
colorful illustrations. But closer examination of the 116
stories reveals that Watchtower writers have added a

unique twist to many. This is true especially of those taken from the New Testament, but even the story on creation taken from Genesis teaches children that, "the first angel God made was very special. He was God's first Son" (story number 1—pages are not numbered).

Concerning the visit of the wise men to the baby Jesus, the story "Men Guided by a Star" concludes that "Satan is the one who must have made that star shine" (story number 86). The story "Jesus is Killed" (number 101) shows him nailed to an upright stake rather than a cross. And number 102 titled "Jesus Is Alive" explains the resurrection of Christ this way:

> Do you know what happened to Jesus' body? God caused it to disappear. God did not raise Jesus to life in the fleshly body in which he died. He gave Jesus a new spirit body, as the angels in heaven have. But to show his disciples he is alive, Jesus can take on a body that people can see, as we will learn.

The book concludes by telling children, "God wants you to live forever on earth in a paradise" (story number 115), but "we need to know about Jehovah and his Son Jesus if we are to live forever," and "no matter how young you are, you are not too young to serve Jehovah" (story number 116).

The February 8, 1981, *Awake!* reported that, "in less than three years this highly popular book has been translated into over 35 languages and printed in some 15 million copies!" (p. 14). Most of these and of the additional millions printed since then are in the hands of non-Witness children. The *1985 Yearbook of Jehovah's Witnesses* (p. 17) tells of a teacher at a Catholic school ordering thirty books for her students, and *Awake!* tells of a Baptist Sunday school superintendent ordering a similar quantity (Jan. 22, 1985, p. 21). Since my wife found (and removed) a copy from the children's library shelves of the Christian elementary school where she teaches, I can believe the JW claims that they have distributed *My Book of Bible Stories* through unsuspecting Christian educators.

Choosing the Best Way of Life, 1979

Directed primarily at Witnesses themselves and new converts, this commentary on Peter's letters outlines their responsibility to study, to preach, to maintain standards of sexual morality, and to submit to organizational authority.

Choosing the Best Way of Life was written by Watchtower headquarters staff member Reinhard Lengtat, according to former Governing Body member Raymond Franz in his book *Crisis of Conscience* (Commentary Press, 1983, p. 228).

Commentary on the Letter of James, 1979

The only Watchtower book to include the word *commentary* in its title, *Commentary on the Letter of James* also comes closest to what non-Witnesses are accustomed to find in a Bible commentary on the shelves of a Christian bookstore. Verses from James are reproduced in small print at the tops of the pages and are then broken down into phrases, which serve as subheadings for discussion. And the "Questions for Study" at the end of each chapter refer to the Bible verses rather than to paragraphs in the book. Moreover, in a further departure from Jehovah's Witness tradition, the writer of this commentary endeavors to present what he understands to be the original meaning and intent of the disciple James in his letter, rather than use James's words as a jumping-off point for modern applications and prophetic speculation.

Commentary on the Letter of James was written by Ed Dunlap, according to former Governing Body member Raymond Franz in his book *Crisis of Conscience* (Commentary Press, 1983, p. 228). Dunlap had served prominently for decades as an instructor at the highest levels of the Watchtower organization, responsible for teaching missionaries and men who run the Society's foreign branch offices. But his frank honesty and his adherence to the Bible rather than organizational tradition led to his being convicted of apostasy by a Watchtower judicial committee in 1980, and to his expulsion from the sect a year after his book was released (*Crisis of Conscience,* pp. 236–289).

Perhaps as an evidence of Dunlap's departure from Watchtower thinking, on page 47 the *Commentary* speaks of all believers receiving a new birth as spirit-begotten sons of God, that is, their being born again: "Besides being the God of Christians, Jehovah is also their Father, for he has begotten them by means of his spirit to be his sons." This conflicts with the organization's teaching that only a very small "anointed class" of believers are spirit begotten as sons of God—fewer than one-tenth of 1 percent, or around eight thousand of the 10 million who attend JW meetings today. Although Dunlap's deviation from official doctrine found its way into print, an article in *The Watchtower* of January 15, 1981 (p. 31), corrects the *Commentary* by suggesting the insertion of "the word 'anointed' in this sentence on the bottom of page 47," so that it will say "anointed Christians" rather than Christians in general.

Speaking freely with me, on the condition that I would not quote him by name, a highly placed Watchtower writer, who chose to remain with the organization but was unhappy with the purge of liberals, told me in 1981 that censorship of publications had been tightened considerably by then and that even some magazine articles he had written during the 1970s would not have made it into print after 1980.

Happiness—How to Find It, 1980
Arguments for the existence of God and for the divine inspiration of the Bible fill the first few chapters of this book, which is obviously intended as a tool for converting nonreligious people. Other chapters demonstrate the

Bible's practicality as a guide in coping with life's problems in such matters as family life, sex, finances, and health. Then toward the end the book narrows its focus, attacks all other religions, and encourages the reader to study and fellowship with Jehovah's Witnesses to survive the imminent end of this world and live on to enjoy paradise restored.

Happiness—How to Find It was written by Watchtower headquarters staff member Gene Smalley, according to former Governing Body member Raymond Franz in his book *Crisis of Conscience* (Commentary Press, 1983, p. 253). But he gives no biographical information about him aside from the fact that this was his first book.

New World Translation of the Holy Scriptures, 1981

Please see the discussion of the 1961 edition in the previous chapter.

Not actually a revision in the true sense, the 1981 edition of the New World Translation is the product of entering the 1970 and 1971 versions into a computer, comparing variations between the two, and selecting the preferred reading. An article in the December 15, 1981, *Watchtower* magazine describes in detail how this Bible was produced by use of the new technologies of computer typesetting and offset printing.

"Let Your Kingdom Come," 1981

Full-color pictures add reader appeal to this book, which otherwise presents the same message as less-colorful volumes published during prior years. Jesus' parables on the kingdom of God are discussed, Old Testament prophecies foretelling the Messiah are considered, and the Watchtower Society's end-times chronology is reviewed. The book for the most part restates old material in a more attractive format.

Of special interest, however, is the "Appendix to Chapter 14" beginning on page 186, which attempts to establish

607 B.C. as the time of Jerusalem's desolation by the Baby-
lonians, in spite of the fact that secular historians generally
assign a date twenty years later. This is an important issue
for Jehovah's Witnesses, because their belief that Christ
returned invisibly as King in A.D. 1914 is based on their
calculations that this would happen 2520 years after
Jerusalem's desolation. (The mathematical arguments are
found on page 135.) So, if 607 B.C. is wrong, then A.D. 1914
is wrong. And if 1914 is wrong, then the entire system of
Watchtower eschatology based on that date falls like a house
of cards. A thorough examination of the question requires
in-depth study of Babylonian inscriptions, astronomical
records, and other chronological data—beyond our present
space limitations and well beyond what most readers would
have patience for. Ex-Witness Carl Olof Jonsson addresses
the Watchtower arguments directly in his book *The Gentile
Times Reconsidered* (Atlanta: Commentary Press, 1986).

You Can Live Forever in Paradise on Earth, 1982

As soon as it was issued, this large, colorfully illustrated volume replaced *The Truth That Leads to Eternal
Life* (1968) as the primary study text for use with prospective converts. In many places it follows the *Truth* book's
argumentation and occasionally even the exact wording,
so that it might almost be considered an expanded and col-
orized version of that earlier book. Within fifteen months
of its release nearly 15 million copies had been printed in
55 languages (*The Watchtower*, January 1, 1984, p. 28). A
pocket-size edition was also printed in 1985 by simple pho-
toreduction of the pages without resetting the type.

Chapter 23 titled "God's Visible Organization" boldly
asserts that "in our day Jesus Christ foretold that there would
be only one source of spiritual instruction for God's people"
(p. 193). It says that instruction comes from "the headquarters of Jehovah's Witnesses in Brooklyn, New York,"
where there is a "governing body, like the apostles and older
men in Jerusalem" (p. 195). This is, in effect, a claim of apos-

tolic succession for the approximately twelve men of the Governing Body. But when apostolic succession is applied to the Roman Catholic Church, JWs are taught that "the doctrine that the 12 apostles have successors to whom authority has been passed by divine appointment" is "not a Bible teaching" (*Reasoning from the Scriptures*, p. 37).

The reader who looks closely at the artwork in this book may be surprised to discover that there are hidden pictures in some of the drawings—grotesque skull faces lurking in the waterfall on page 93, for example, and a human skeleton dangling from the trees on page 144. These, together with dozens of other faces and satanic symbols concealed in Watchtower illustrations during the 1980s point to a pattern of occult subversion according to a book by ex-Witness Darek Barefoot. In *Jehovah's Witnesses and the Hour of Darkness: Occult Subversion and Blind Faith in the Watchtower Society* he tells how a curly-headed bearded face clearly visible on a woman's skirt in the February 1, 1983, *Watchtower* magazine (p. 17) triggered letters to the Brooklyn headquarters, only to be met by denials from the sect's leadership. Then *The Watchtower* of September 1, 1984, condemned "rumors—for example, that one of the artists had secretly been introducing pictures of demons into the illustrations," labeling such reports "false" (p. 20). And the March 1, 1987, *Watchtower* assured readers that "every page, including the artwork, is scrutinized by selected members of the Governing Body before it is printed" (p. 15). See also the discussion of illustrations in the 1988 book *Revelation—Its Grand Climax At Hand!*

A revised edition of *You Can Live Forever in Paradise on Earth* was released in 1989. Concerning this the December 1989 issue of *Our Kingdom Ministry* states (p. 7):

> The only significant change is with regard to the Sodomites, on pages 178 and 179. This change appeared in the *Revelation* book, page 273, and in *The Watchtower* of June 1, 1988, pages 30 and 31. You may wish to note it in earlier printings that you have on hand.

This new edition reverses the Watchtower Society's teaching on whether the inhabitants of Sodom and Gomorrah will be resurrected. On page 179 the millions of copies printed prior to the change state that at Matthew 10:15 "Jesus showed that at least some of the unrighteous people of ancient Sodom and Gomorrah will be present on earth during Judgment Day . . . we can expect that some of them will be resurrected." The revised editions say instead that "the people of Sodom and of the surrounding cities suffered a destruction from which they will apparently never be resurrected."

Interestingly, this is not the first time that Jehovah's Witnesses have reversed themselves on the fate of the Sodomites. The *Watchtower* magazine's answer to the question of whether these people will be resurrected was *yes* in the issue of July 1879 (p. 8), *no* in that of June 1, 1952 (p. 338), *yes* again in the issue of August 1, 1965 (p. 479), and *no* once more in that of June 1, 1988 (p. 31). This proves useful when JWs attempt to justify other doctrinal changes by saying that their "light gets brighter." On this question their light has evidently been blinking on and off.

Another change of less significance was made in *You Can Live Forever in Paradise on Earth* shortly after it was released. In copies printed for release at JW conventions (with the title page preceded by a letter addressed "Dear Kingdom Publishers"), the paragraph subtitled "Seek Your Mate's Pleasure" on the lower half of page 244 is accompanied by a full-color illustration of a woman alone wearing a bathrobe and seated with her feet pulled up on what appears to be the end of a bed. Behind her left shoulder is an end table holding a lamp and a telephone. But in other printings that are similarly labeled "First Edition: 5,000,000 Copies," the same woman is dressed in a blouse and skirt and seated on a stuffed chair. Her husband is standing behind her right shoulder, and the end table holds a lamp, a vase of flowers, and a ram's-head plaque. No explanation was offered, but some Witnesses who noticed the difference in these early copies speculated at the time that those with the ram's head were actually printed first and that the illustration was then altered to remove what they viewed as a pagan symbol. However, later printings and the 1989 revised edition continue to feature the ram's head.

As of this writing Jehovah's Witnesses are still using *You Can Live Forever in Paradise on Earth* as the standard text to study with potential converts.

Organized to Accomplish Our Ministry, 1983

This replaced *Organization for Kingdom-Preaching and Disciple-Making* (1972) as a handbook for elders and ministerial servants in caring for congregation meetings, house-to-house preaching, and judicial matters. It also contains a new catechism of more than one hundred questions for baptismal candidates. The book is not distributed to outsiders but only to Witnesses themselves and new disciples approaching baptism. Reflecting tightened organizational control following the purge of 1980–81, it warns them, "This is no time for independent thinking" (p. 8)—a theme further elaborated on in the January 15, 1983, *Watchtower* under subheadings "Avoid Independent Thinking" (p. 22) and "Fight Against Independent Thinking" (p. 27).

United in Worship of the Only True God, 1983

This pocket-size volume serves as a second book for new converts to study after they have completed *You Can Live Forever in Paradise on Earth* and prior to being baptized as full-fledged Jehovah's Witnesses. It reviews basic doctrines, discusses "The Meaning of Your Baptism," takes a closer look at the organization, and sets out what is required in the way of personal conduct and preaching activity.

One matter mentioned here that the organization has seldom put into print elsewhere, perhaps to avoid legal problems, is the expectation that Witnesses will not only refuse military service but will also decline "to do non-combatant service or to accept other work assignments as a substitute for military service" (p. 167).

New World Translation of the Holy Scriptures (revised), 1984

Please see the discussion of the 1961 edition in the previous chapter.

New World Translation of the Holy Scriptures—With References, 1984

This large volume contains the 1984 revision (see above) with the addition of marginal cross references and extensive footnotes.

Survival Into a New Earth, 1984

Attention is drawn here to forty-seven "Prophectic Patterns and Descriptions of People Now Living Who Will Inherit the Earthly Realm of God's Kingdom" (p. 190). From beginning to end the book presents the end of the world as imminent and holds before the reader the hope of surviving that catastrophic event. Chapter 3 titled "How Long Will the Present System Last?" concludes that Christ returned invisibly and began "to rule as King in 1914 and that the end of this wicked world would come within the generation that saw the beginning of these things" (p. 25). Chapter 16 "What Will You Personally Do?" warns the reader that "there is no time to lose" and to take the steps required for survival now "during the final days of this system of things" (p. 128). And the last chapter brings the sense of urgency to a peak with its title "The Countdown Nears Its Zero Hour!"

Sing Praises to Jehovah, 1984

Musically the book of 225 songs released in 1984 differs from earlier versions in that it provides notations for guitar. But more significant is the different doctrinal emphasis commented on in the Watchtower Society's book Revelation—Its Grand Climax At Hand!

In the songbook produced by Jehovah's people in 1905, there were twice as many songs praising Jesus as there were songs praising Jehovah God. In their 1928 songbook, the number of songs extolling Jesus was about the same as the number extolling Jehovah. But in the latest songbook of 1984, Jehovah is honored by four times as many songs as is Jesus. This is in harmony with Jesus' own words: "The Father is greater than I am." (John 14:28) Love for Jehovah must be preeminent, accompanied by deep love for Jesus and appreciation of his precious sacrifice and office as God's High Priest and King. (p. 36)

This comment reveals that Watchtower leaders are well aware that the organization's doctrinal shifts over the years have made it far less Christ centered, and that this changed emphasis is reflected in its songs of worship. But what the quotation fails to reveal is that the shift away from Jesus Christ has been accompanied by a growing emphasis on the organization, which itself takes on the role of a corporate false Christ obeyed as master and looked to for salvation.

Hints of this can be found in a number of the newer songs. For example, song number 8 in the 1984 book is titled "Loyally Submitting to Theocratic Order," and its third and final stanza begins

Then we have God's "steward" and His active force.
These will ever guide us in our Christian course.

Witnesses who sing these verses understand "God's 'steward'" to be a term much like *vicar of Christ* applied to the Watchtower leadership, giving them authority like that of the popes of the Middle Ages. (The term *active force* is the Watchtower's impersonal designation for the Holy Spirit.) Note, too, these words from song number 38 titled "Displaying Loyalty":

To God's loyal congregation We too will show loyalty,
Give it our steadfast allegiance Even in adversity,

Also, these from number 42, "This is the Way":

> He has a fine channel that's surely unique,
> And thru it he chooses to warn and to speak.

Such verses, sung with deep conviction, continually impress upon Jehovah's Witnesses that the organization speaks for God and that loyalty to God is manifested by loyal allegiance to the organization.

Even the songs that do focus on Christ, such as number 105, "Hail Jehovah's Firstborn!" lower him to the status of a created being:

> Let's hail Jehovah's Firstborn—God's Heir he has been made—
> Who since he was created, His Father's voice obeyed.

So, while most Christians might have felt comfortable singing from the hymnal Charles Taze Russell produced for his followers in 1879, such would hardly be the case with the songbook Jehovah's Witnesses use today.

The Kingdom Interlinear Translation of the Greek Scriptures (revised), 1985

Please see the discussion of the original 1969 edition.

The 1985 revised edition employs the 1984 revision of the New World Translation in the English column. It also stands half an inch shorter than the original and is closer to pocket size. A notable change in the interlinear column is found at Colossians 2:9, where *theotes* is given the rendering "divinity" instead of "godship" as in the first edition. The appendix is also greatly expanded with additional articles that support the Watchtower Society's unusual renderings.

Life—How Did It Get Here? By Evolution or by Creation? 1985

With an abundance of colorful illustrations this large volume updates and replaces *Did Man Get Here by Evolution or by Creation?* (1967). It presents a powerful attack on the theory of evolution, together with a masterful defense of the Bible and its creation account. But it also subtly weaves in attacks on "conventional religion" (p. 184) and arguments that advance Jehovah's Witnesses as the one true religion, especially in the final chapters. And the closing discussion urges the reader to "conform to Jehovah's requirements" to embrace this hope: "What a glorious prospect—living forever on a Paradise earth—if you make the right choice!" (pp. 250–251).

Reasoning From the Scriptures, 1985

This reference work replaced *"Make Sure of All Things: Hold Fast to What Is Fine"* (1965) as a source of proof texts for Jehovah's Witnesses to use in justifying their beliefs and attacking those of other religious groups. But this book goes beyond the scope of its predecessor by providing not merely Scripture verses but also clever responses and lines of argument to use in discussions with outsiders. These are presented under the heading "If Someone Says—" at the end of many of the chapters.

For example, at the end of the chapter on "False Prophets" are three suggested replies to use "If Someone Says—'My minister said that Jehovah's Witnesses are the false prophets'" (p. 137). And at the conclusion of the chapter on the New World Translation are several suggestions as to how to respond if someone says, accusingly, "You have your own Bible" (p. 279).

Many proposed responses are tricky, or perhaps even deceptive, and are designed to overcome a householder's objections and permit the Witness to continue with a prepared presentation. Thus, on page 360 the book suggests:

> *If Someone Says—'I'm saved'*
> *You might reply:* 'I am glad to know that, because it tells me that you believe in Jesus Christ. The work in which I am sharing is one that Jesus assigned his followers to do.'

In actuality the JW views "saved" Christians as enslaved by the devil, and he is not at all glad about this claim of salvation; but he is glad to *know* what his listener thinks, and uses this as a jumping-off point for the remainder of his rehearsed speech.

Similarly, although the millions of Jehovah's Witnesses have been taught that they cannot be born again, but that this privilege is reserved for an elite group of some eight thousand people on earth today, they are encouraged to give this reply to an outsider who asks, "Have you been born again?"

> You want to know whether I have accepted Jesus as my Savior and have received holy spirit, is that right? May I assure you that the answer is Yes; otherwise I would not be talking to you about Jesus. (p. 79)

With their weekly training in the use of such evasive maneuvers and carefully thought-out arguments, it is no wonder that Jehovah's Witnesses are so difficult to deal with when they call at the home. Even Christians who are well read in the Bible find that they are no match for these visitors who have rehearsed not only their own presentations but also the Christians' anticipated responses and how they will answer them. The existence of such a book as *Reasoning from the Scriptures* in the hands of Jehovah's Witnesses highlights the need for Christians contemplating dialogue with them to prepare thoroughly ahead of time. Otherwise, there is a real danger not only of losing the argument but also of falling victim to the Witnesses' carefully orchestrated efforts to convert their listeners.

Those who confidently say to themselves, "It could never happen to me," are often in the greatest danger. I expressed the same overconfidence just before embarking on my own thirteen years in the sect. And while I was a member I knew personally a man who had been a deacon in a Baptist church when JWs began conducting a study with his wife. The deacon sat in on the study to prove the Witnesses wrong, but they convinced him instead. He and his wife both left the Baptist church and joined Jehovah's Witnesses, remaining in the sect until they died several years later.

There are good, solid answers Christians can give to refute everything the Watchtower teaches, but they require study and preparation. Going up against the Witnesses without prior training can prove disastrous.

True Peace and Security—How Can You Find It? 1986

This is a revised version of the 1973 book *True Peace and Security—From What Source?* with many colorful illustrations added and the text updated. Just as release of the original volume heightened expectations of the world's end by the year 1975, this new release in 1986 stirred up such hopes for the year 1986 itself. A sense of urgency was conveyed by the fact that the book was released at a special talk at kingdom halls across the United States on March 9, 1986, rather than at the usual time for book releases during the summer Watchtower conventions.

The revised text starts out with an ominous reference to the fact that "the United Nations declared 1986 an 'International Year of Peace'" with "the goal of 'peace, international security and cooperation'" (p.5), words Jehovah's Witnesses had already been taught to view as a final signal of the world's end. Then, under the heading "A Final Signal" on page 85, it says concerning the United Nations declaration, "This, no doubt, is a step toward the fulfillment of Paul's above-quoted words" from 1 Thessalonians 5:2, 3, which say that "sudden destruction is to be instantly upon them" (NWT).

Worldwide Security Under the "Prince of Peace," 1986

Taking full advantage of the preprogrammed reaction of Jehovah's Witnesses to the expression "peace and security" (see the discussion of *True Peace and Security—How Can You Find It?* above), the Watchtower Society issued in 1986 a second book employing those key words in its title.

Written primarily for Jehovah's Witnesses themselves, it reviews the Society's interpretation of many Bible prophecies as having fulfillment in events taking place with respect to the Watchtower organization from 1914 onward. Why did much of the world go to war in that year? This book explains:

> When Jehovah's Kingdom was set up in the heavens in 1914, the nations raged in opposition to that Kingdom by engaging in the first world war. . . . Satan the Devil endeavored to use that world conflict to destroy the visible part of Jehovah's organization. He succeeded in having the president of the Watch Tower Bible and Tract Society imprisoned in the federal penitentiary in Atlanta, Georgia. (p. 145)

This pocket-size volume also reflects an organizational emphasis in chapters that bear such titles as "Loyally Remembering Jehovah's Organization" (17) and "Loyalty to God's Visible Organization Today" (18).

But perhaps the most interesting expression in the book is the one employed on page 169 to answer this study question: "Into what new relationship toward the human race will Jehovah God come?" The response is that "the heavenly Father of Jesus Christ will become the heavenly Grandfather of the restored human family."

Yearbook (without daily texts), 1986

Breaking with the tradition established back in 1927, the Society began once again publishing the annual *Yearbook of Jehovah's Witnesses* without daily Scripture texts and discussions. These were produced separately as a booklet titled *Examining the Scriptures Daily.*

Watch Tower Publications Index 1930–1985, 1986

This is the first cumulative *Index* published since the one released in 1961, which covered the period from 1930 through 1960. In the interim an annual index was produced each year, and five-year indexes were released in 1976 (for 1971–1975) and in 1981 (for 1976–1980).

This cumulative index follows the same pattern as the previous one in omitting certain embarrassing references. For example, although the 1966–1970 five-year index lists under "Cannibalism" the November 15, 1967, *Watchtower,* p. 702, which banned organ transplants as a form of cannibalism, the 1930–1985 cumulative index, produced after the ban was lifted, omits that listing. Similarly, under "Transplanting, body parts, Witnesses' view," 1967 and 1968 magazine articles banning the practice are listed in the five-year index but omitted entirely in the cumulative index, which lists instead a 1980 article reversing the teaching and allowing transplants.

The headings "Armageddon, nearness of" and "Armageddon, time of" could be expected to feature references to an August 15, 1968, *Watchtower* study article titled "Why Are You Looking Forward to 1975?" (p. 494) that said:

> Are we to assume from this study that the battle of Armageddon will be all over by the autumn of 1975, and the long-looked-for thousand-year reign of Christ will begin by then? . . . It may involve only a difference of weeks or months, not years. (p. 499)

But there is no mention of the article in either place. Nor is the article cited under the main alphabetical heading "1975," nor under "Dates of Prophetic Significance," but only under the obscure heading "Dates, C.E., 1975, six thousand years of man's existence." Similarly, a researcher would have a difficult time using the *Index* to find these other pages naming the year 1975 as a possible or likely time for the end of the world: *The Watchtower,* October 15, 1966, pp. 628–631; May 1, 1967, p. 262; May 1, 1968, pp. 271–273; *Awake!* October 8, 1966, pp. 19–20; October 8, 1968, p. 14.

See also *Watch Tower Publications Index (1930–1960),* 1961.

Insight on the Scriptures, 1988

A two-volume Bible dictionary, *Insight on the Scriptures* was published to replace *Aid to Bible Understanding* (1971). However, it is essentially the same book reset in larger type, with the addition of many colorful illustrations and maps. Most of the articles are taken word for word from *Aid to Bible Understanding.*

Odd as it may seem, the two books released by the Watchtower Society at its summer 1988 conventions contradict each other on the question of whether or not the inhabitants of Sodom and Gomorrah will be resurrected. *Insight on the Scriptures* indicates on page 985 that they will; *Revelation—Its Grand Climax at Hand* says on page 273 that they will not. The teaching was officially changed in the June 1, 1988, *Watchtower* magazine, evidently in time to catch the printing of the latter book but too late for the former. For additional information on this matter, please see the discussion above on the book *You Can Live Forever in Paradise on Earth* (1982).

Revelation—Its Grand Climax at Hand, 1988

The Watchtower Society's first full-color commentary on Revelation asserts about itself that "the entire book of Revelation is explained in this publication" (p. 5). Yet, the verse-by-verse commentary skims over Revelation 22:13. This is significant in that the book elsewhere attempts to make a distinction between the title "the First and the Last" as applied to Jesus in Revelation 1:17 and to Jehovah in Isaiah 44:6. A footnote on page 27 says:

> In the original Hebrew at Isaiah 44:6, there is no definite article with the words "first" and "last," whereas in Jesus' description of himself in the original Greek at Revelation 1:17, the definite article is found. So, grammatically, Revelation 1:17 indicates a title, whereas Isaiah 44:6 describes Jehovah's Godship.

That this reasoning leads to a false distinction, however, becomes obvious when Revelation 1:17 and Revelation 2:8 (both of which call Jesus "the First and the Last") are compared with Revelation 22:13 (which the Witnesses apply to Jehovah God). All three verses use the *identical* expression in Greek (*ho protos kai ho eschatos:* "The first and the last") *with* the definite article. Apparently to avoid having to face this fact, this Watchtower book skims over Revelation 22:13 in its verse-by-verse commentary, discussing verses 12 and 14 without commenting on verse 13 except to say that "Jehovah God emphasizes his eternal sovereignty and the fact that what he first purposes he will at last perform" (p. 316).

Just as *The Finished Mystery* taught in 1917 that the Watchtower organization was being directed from beyond the grave by the late Pastor Russell's departed spirit, *Revelation—Its Grand Climax at Hand* contains a similar reference to communication with the dead. On page 125 it indicates such a source for some of the sect's new truths, claiming that deceased members who are now "resurrected ones" in heaven may be passing information on to the Watchtower leadership:

> Yes, that elder could locate the answer and give it to John. This suggests that resurrected ones of the 24-elders group may be involved in the communicating of divine truths today.

It is also noteworthy that the two books released by the Watchtower Society at its summer 1988 conventions contradict each other on the question of whether or not the inhabitants of Sodom and Gomorrah will be resurrected. Please see the discussion of *Insight on the Scriptures* above.

Some of the artwork in *Revelation—Its Grand Climax At Hand* contains hidden pictures. Particularly obvious are the face in the angel's hand on page 159 and the impish human face that appears on page 91 when the horse's snout is covered—nearly turning this horse into a centaur. These and other concealed drawings in this book and other Watchtower publications give evidence of occult subversion at the sect's Brooklyn headquarters, according to a book by ex-Witness Darek Barefoot, who was disfellow-shipped in connection with his role as a whistle blower. For additional details, see the discussion of the 1982 book *You Can Live Forever in Paradise on Earth*.

The Bible—God's Word or Man's? 1989

With abundantly more illustrations—in full color—but with less text, this replaces the 1969 publication *Is the Bible Really the Word of God?* Unlike its predecessor, which reserves attacks on other churches for the end of the book, *The Bible—God's Word or Man's?* reviles Christendom at every opportunity throughout. But it concludes in the same manner, inviting the reader to turn to Jehovah's Witnesses for help in understanding the Scriptures. In fact, implying that the Bible cannot be understood alone, it gives the example of a woman who "was a regular Bible reader, but there were many important teachings of the Bible that she had not come to understand from her own reading. It was only when she had discussions with Jehovah's Witnesses that she learned of basic Bible truths" (p. 185).

Questions Young People Ask: Answers That Work, 1989

A replacement for *Your Youth—Getting the Best out of It* (1976), this book deals with the same subject matter but enhances the discussions with plentiful full-color photographs of young people in various situations.

Topics covered include depression, problems in the home, dating, drugs and alcohol, school, career choices, sex and morals, peer pressure, and leisure-time activities. Much of the material offers the same advice that a Christian or secular counselor would provide, but some of it carries a unique Watchtower twist. For example, the chapter on career choices encourages young people to decide "against a university education" and to seek part-time employment so they will be free to devote full time to distributing JW literature from door to door (pp. 175–179).

Mankind's Search for God, 1990

In a more colorful format and with updated information, this book presents much of the same material as *What Has Religion Done for Mankind?* (1951). But it devotes considerably more space to Hinduism, Buddhism, Taoism, Confucianism, Shintoism, and Islam—perhaps because there are now one-quarter million Jehovah's Witnesses active in lands where those religions predominate, nearly as many as there were in the lands of Christendom when the earlier book was written.

The discussion of Christianity is strongly slanted to highlight hypocrisy and abuses in other churches while it presents a rosy picture of Jehovah's Witnesses. After asking the rhetorical question, "Where did Jehovah's Witnesses come from?" the chapter titled "A Return to the True God" identifies Cain's brother Abel as "the first witness of Jehovah" and names "Noah, Abraham, Sarah, and Moses" as "further examples of Jehovah's faithful witnesses" (pp. 348–349). "Jesus was a true witness," it says, and then indicates that "Christ's authentic followers down through the ages would likewise be witnesses of him and of the true God, Jehovah" (p. 350).

The account then skips ahead to the year 1870, introducing Charles Taze Russell as a young man whose "religious background was Presbyterian and Congregational" (p.351). It mentions that he "started a weekly Bible study group with other young men," and that he had "collaborators" before starting to publish *Zion's Watch Tower and Herald of Christ's Presence* in 1879 (p. 352). But it completely conceals his ten-year involvement with the Second Adventists, from 1868 through 1878, during which time Russell learned many of his religious concepts from Adventist preachers and writers Jonas Wendell, George Stetson, and George Storrs. In the *Watch Tower* of July 15, 1906, Russell writes, "Thus I confess indebtedness to Adventists," and names these three men as his teachers (p. 3821, reprints).

Also, the account fails to mention that, for some time prior to starting his own magazine, Russell served as one of the assistant editors of the Second Adventist publication *The Herald of the Morning,* and that he used that magazine's mailing list to begin circulating his own. Moreover, this book makes it seem as if Russell and his "Bible Students" were publishing the *Watch Tower* and meeting in their own congregations when "they discovered that Christ's 'coming' was, in fact, a *'pa-rou-sía,'* or *invisible presence"* (p. 353). But other Watchtower histories acknowledge that Russell learned this from Adventist N. H. Barbour in 1876, three years before separating from Barbour's Adventist group and starting his own magazine (*Jehovah's Witnesses in the Divine Purpose,* p. 18; *Zion's Watch Tower,* July 15, 1906, p. 3822, reprints).

For most readers of *Mankind's Search for God,* the Watchtower Society's version of its own history presented here will stand unchallenged. But well-informed readers will find this far-from-frank presentation of its origins to be sufficient reason to question the sect's claim to be the only religion teaching the truth.

"All Scripture Is Inspired of God and Beneficial," 1990

This is a new edition of the book by the same title published in 1963, with very little textual revision. The new printing features a modern typeface and a bit more artwork.

The Greatest Man Who Ever Lived, 1991

With an initial printing of more than 12 million copies, this book was released more or less simultaneously in some sixty languages. This was possible because it consists of material that originally appeared in serial form in 149 consecutive issues of *The Watchtower* in those languages, beginning in April 1985.

An article announcing the book says that "in effect, *The Greatest Man Who Ever Lived* provides a commentary on the Gospels." It also notes that "an effort was made to present every speech Jesus delivered and every recorded event in his earthly life," and that "everything is related in chronological order" (*The Watchtower,* February 15, 1992, pp. 19–20).

Page numbers cannot be cited since, strangely, the 448 pages in this book are not numbered. But the division into 133 chapters, plus introductory material, means that chapters average fewer than four pages in length, thus facilitating reference by chapter number.

Unsuspecting recipients of this colorfully illustrated volume will assume that it faithfully presents the story of Jesus. But the story is given a unique slant, as can be seen from the following examples. According to the introductory chapter, "Jesus never claimed to be God, but he acknowledged that he was the promised Messiah, or Christ. He also said he was 'God's Son,' *not God"* (emphasis theirs). Chapter 7, titled "Jesus and the Astrologers," explains that "Satan provided the star" that guided visitors from the East first to Jerusalem and then to the baby Jesus in Bethlehem. Chapter 80 interprets Jesus' remarks at Luke 12:32 and John 10:16 by saying, "This little flock, which eventually numbers 144,000 . . . will rule with Christ in heaven, and the 'other sheep' in the other fold will live on the Paradise earth." Chapter 132 asserts that "it was in 1914 that Jesus returned invisibly." And chapter 125 changes the meaning of Christ's words to the evildoer crucified next to him by breaking up the sentence this way: "'Truly I tell you today,' Jesus replies, 'You will be with me in Paradise.'" Thus, the man's arrival in Paradise is postponed from "today," as Jesus' words indicate in most Bibles, to some future time during Christ's thousand-year reign:

> No, that man will not be taken to heaven to rule as a king with Jesus, nor will Jesus again become a man and live on the Para-

dise earth with him. Rather, Jesus will be with the former evil-doer in the sense that He will resurrect him to life in Paradise and see to it that his needs, both physical and spiritual, are cared for. (Ch. 133)

So, although millions around the earth will learn about "Jesus" through this book, it is not exactly the same Jesus revealed in the Bible.

Booklets

Watchtower booklets, almost too numerous to mention, are simply listed here. Only those of lasting significance are discussed. Many are simply printed transcripts of talks given at major conventions.

Jehovah's Witnesses in the Twentieth Century, 1978

This brochure promoting the Watchtower organization was also reissued in a revised edition in 1979.

Unseen Spirits—Do They Help Us? Or Do They Harm Us? 1978

"Pay Attention to Yourselves and to All the Flock" (second booklet), 1979

This served as the textbook for a training program for elders. Circulation of the booklet was limited to the elders themselves.

The Path of Divine Truth Leading to Liberation, 1980

"Pay Attention to Yourselves and to All the Flock" (third booklet), 1981

This served as the textbook for a training program for elders. Circulation of the booklet was limited to the elders themselves.

Enjoy Life on Earth Forever! 1982

Dwelling Together in Unity (revised), 1982

From Kurukshetra to Armageddon, 1983

School and Jehovah's Witnesses, 1983

Produced for JW parents to give to their children's public school teachers, this large thirty-two page booklet spells out Watchtower policies restricting youngsters from participation in organized sports, school dances, elective offices, holiday celebrations, sex education classes, flag ceremonies, and the singing or playing of patriotic or religious music.

In Search of a Father, 1983

Good News for All Nations, 1983

With a one-page introduction to the message of Jehovah's Witnesses in each of fifty-nine languages, this booklet replaces "*Preach the Word*" (1953).

The Time for True Submission to God, 1983

Centennial of the Watch Tower Bible and Tract Society of Pennsylvania, 1984

It is of interest that the Watchtower organization observes its own centennial but prohibits followers from observing birthday celebrations.

The Divine Name That Will Endure Forever, 1984

This booklet presents arguments for the use of the name Jehovah in worship and for its insertion in the New Testament.

The Government That Will Bring Paradise, 1985

Examining the Scriptures Daily, 1986

Commencing in 1986 the Society resumed the pre-1927 practice of publishing the annual *Yearbook of Jehovah's Witnesses* without daily Scripture texts and discussions. These were removed from the *Yearbook* and published separately in the form of this booklet.

"Look! I Am Making All Things New," 1986

A thirty-two-page brochure the size of a *Watchtower* magazine, this booklet features large, easy-to-read type. It is designed as a tool for starting studies with newly interested individuals who are not good readers.

Jehovah's Witnesses—Unitedly Doing God's Will Worldwide, 1986

This thirty-two-page brochure the same size as a *Watchtower* or *Awake!* magazine focuses on the contemporary organization of Jehovah's Witnesses. Colorful photos impress the reader with the sect's massive printing operations and its international character.

Should You Believe in the Trinity? 1989

With its clever arguments and out-of-context quotations from early Christian-church writings and other sources, this thirty-two-page booklet has sent many Christians reeling and has turned many other people against trinitarian churches. Refutation can be found in *Why You Should Believe in the Trinity,* by Robert M. Bowman, Jr. and *Exposing "Should You Believe in the Trinity?"* by Angel Arellano.

How Can Blood Save Your Life? 1990

Biblical and medical arguments are presented here to support the Watchtower Society's ban on blood transfusions for its followers and their minor children. The discussion is intended to persuade outsiders, particularly medical personnel, to respect the position Jehovah's Witnesses take on the matter. (Witnesses themselves know that they will be put on trial before a committee of elders and will be expelled from the sect and shunned by fellow believers if they permit blood to be administered to themselves or their children.)

The booklet acknowledges that "court cases regarding blood mainly involve children" (p. 21). But it reproduces a magazine article stating that Jehovah's Witnesses "gladly cooperate with physicians and medical staff" (p. 29). This leaves the reader with the impression that JWs will allow their children to receive transfusions ordered by a court.

However, other literature aimed at Witnesses themselves instructs them to "resist a blood transfusion that has been ordered or authorized by a court." They are advised to "avoid being accessible" for such a court-ordered transfusion by fleeing the scene, or else to follow the example of a twelve-year-old girl who had been taught to "fight any court-authorized transfusion with all the strength she could muster, that she would scream and struggle, that she would pull the injecting device out of her arm and would attempt to destroy the blood in the bag over her bed" (*The Watchtower,* June 15, 1991, p. 31). This article advises that this course be followed even if such action might make the Jehovah's Witness "a lawbreaker or make him liable to prosecution" by the authorities.

Pay Attention to Yourselves and to All the Flock, 1991

Subtitled *Kingdom Ministry School Textbook,* this revises and consolidates into 158 pages the three booklets of lessons for elders issued under the same title in 1977, 1979, and 1981. A box on the title page explains that an elder who has taken the course may retain the booklet as long as he continues to serve in that capacity, but if he loses his appointed position he must then turn over his copy to the committee of elders in charge of his local congregation.

Tracts and Pamphlets

Watchtower tracts and pamphlets of the Franz era are simply listed here.

Kingdom News No. 25 (Why Are We Here?), 1978

Kingdom News No. 26 (Relief From Pressure—Is It Possible?), 1978

Kingdom News No. 27 (What Has Happened to Love?),
1979

Kingdom News No. 28 (Hope for Ending Inflation, Sickness, Crime, War?), 1980

Kingdom News No. 29 (Is a Happy Life Really Possible?),
1981

Kingdom News No. 30 (Is Planet Earth Near the Brink?),
1981

Kingdom News No. 31 (Are We Nearing Armageddon?),
1982

This is, in essence, an advertisement for the *Watchtower* and *Awake!* magazines, and it concludes with a subscription appeal and order form.

Kingdom News No. 32 (A United Happy Family—What Is the Key?), 1983

Kingdom News No. 33 (Life—How Did It Get Here? By Evolution or by Creation?), 1985

How to Find the Road to Paradise, 1990

Prominently featuring quotations from the Koran, this tract introduces Muslims to the Watchtower message.

A Peaceful New World—Will It Come? 1991

According to *Our Kingdom Ministry* (p. 7) of February 1992 this tract targets "the Jewish population" in particular.

Does God Really Care About Us?: Will This World Survive? 1992

Comfort for the Depressed, 1992

Enjoy Family Life, 1992

Who Really Rules the World? 1992

7

The Milton G. Henschel Era Begins

President
December 30, 1992

An era ended abruptly with the fourth Watchtower president's death on December 22, 1992. Frederick W. Franz was ninety-nine years old and died of a heart attack. He had strongly influenced the content of Jehovah's Witness literature for nearly half a century.

His successor was chosen on December 30, 1992: Milton G. Henschel, age 72, the Society's long-time vice president. Born in Pomona, New Jersey, near Atlantic City, Henschel is a third-generation JW and has lived and worked at the sect's Brooklyn headquarters complex for some fifty years.

Very little has ever been written about the new man. Former Governing Body member Raymond Franz describes him in his book *Crisis of Conscience* as an administrator overseeing the organization's printing factories but leaving much of their printed output unread. If this is so, Henschel may follow Nathan Knorr's example in leaving doctrinal matters to underlings.

Still, regardless of the role Milton Henschel may play in it, fundamental change can be expected in the content of Jehovah's Witness literature, since much of the doctrine developed by the late Fred Franz revolved around the generation that "saw the events of 1914"—the generation of his contemporaries who have, for the most part, joined him in leaving this world. New material published under Henschel can be expected to replace failed prophecies and outdated chronologies with biblical interpretations more relevant to Jehovah's Witnesses today.

8

Watchtower Bible Commentaries

Although most Watchtower literature presents doctrine topically and cites proof texts scattered throughout the Bible, several books take the form of biblical commentaries that cover portions of Scripture in traditional verse-by-verse fashion. Where successive publications have expounded on the same biblical passages, comparison reveals much about the development of Watchtower doctrine over the years. Such books are identified here to facilitate comparison.

Commentaries on Ruth

Preservation, 1932, covers the entire Book of Ruth, as well as Esther.

Commentaries on Esther

Preservation, 1932, covers the entire Book of Esther, as well as Ruth.

Commentaries on Job

Life, 1929, covers the Book of Job from beginning to end, but skips many verses.

The New World, 1942, covers the Book of Job from beginning to end, but skips many verses.

Commentaries on Song of Solomon

The Finished Mystery (Studies in the Scriptures, Volume 7), 1917, covers the entire Song of Solomon, as well as Ezekiel and Revelation.

Commentaries on Isaiah

"Babylon the Great Has Fallen!" God's Kingdom Rules! 1963, covers Isaiah, chapters 13, 14, 21, 43–48, 51:17–52:12, as well as portions of Jeremiah, Daniel, and Revelation.

Commentaries on Jeremiah

"Babylon the Great Has Fallen!" God's Kingdom Rules! 1963, covers Jeremiah, chapters 50 and 51, as well as portions of Isaiah, Daniel, and Revelation.

Commentaries on Ezekiel

The Finished Mystery (Studies in the Scriptures, Volume 7), 1917, covers the entire Book of Ezekiel, as well as Song of Solomon and Revelation.

Vindication (Book One), 1931, covers Ezekiel, chapters 1–24.

Vindication (Book Two), 1932, covers Ezekiel, chapters 25–39.

Vindication (Book Three), 1932, covers Ezekiel, chapters 40–48, as well as Haggai and portions of Zechariah.

"The Nations Shall Know That I Am Jehovah"—How?
1971, covers Ezekiel from beginning to end but omits discussion of chapters 5, 12–20, 22, 25–32, 35, 41, 42, and 44–46.

Commentaries on Daniel

Light, Book Two, 1930, covers portions of Daniel, chapter 2, as well as portions of Revelation.

Our Incoming World Government—God's Kingdom, 1977, although not set up as a verse-by-verse commentary, comments in detail on much of chapters 2, 4, 7, and 12 of the Book of Daniel.

"Your Will Be Done on Earth," 1958, although not set up as a verse-by-verse commentary, discusses chapters 7, 8, 11, and 12 of the Book of Daniel.

"Babylon the Great Has Fallen!" God's Kingdom Rules! 1963, covers portions of Daniel, chapter 5, as well as portions of Isaiah, Jeremiah, and Revelation.

Commentaries on Joel

Religion, 1940, covers the entire Book of Joel.

Commentaries on Haggai

Vindication (Book Three), 1932, covers all of Haggai, as well as portions of Ezekiel and Zechariah.

Paradise Restored to Mankind—By Theocracy! 1972, covers all of Haggai, as well as Zechariah.

Commentaries on Zechariah

Vindication (Book Three), 1932, covers portions of Zechariah, chapter 3, as well as Haggai and portions of Ezekiel.

Preparation, 1933, covers the entire Book of Zechariah.

Paradise Restored to Mankind—By Theocracy! 1972, covers all of Zechariah, as well as Haggai.

Commentaries on the Gospels

The Greatest Man Who Ever Lived, 1991, is not a traditional verse-by-verse commentary but covers the life of Christ in chronological fashion, with references to the appropriate verses of the four Gospels.

Commentaries on the Letter of James

Commentary on James, 1979, covers all of James.

Commentaries on Peter

Choosing the Best Way of Life, 1979, covers First and Second Peter.

Commentaries on Revelation

The Finished Mystery (Studies in the Scriptures, Volume 7), 1917, covers the entire Book of Revelation, as well as Song of Solomon and Ezekiel.

Light (Book One), 1930, covers Revelation, chapters 1–14.

Light (Book Two), 1930, covers Revelation, chapters 15–22, as well as portions of Daniel.

"Babylon the Great Has Fallen!" God's Kingdom Rules! 1963, covers Revelation, chapters 14–22, as well as portions of Isaiah, Jeremiah, and Daniel.

"Then Is Finished the Mystery of God," 1969, covers Revelation, chapters 1–13.

Revelation—Its Grand Climax at Hand, 1988, covers virtually all of Revelation.

Commentaries on the Entire Bible

"All Scripture Is Inspired of God and Beneficial," 1963, and 1990 revision, contains a brief commentary on each book of the Bible.

Organizational Names

Adventist(s)   This name was first applied to followers of Baptist lay preacher William Miller, who had predicted Christ would return in October 1843 or 1844. After
the great "Disappointment of 1844," Miller's followers
formed several Adventist sects. Watchtower founder
Charles T. Russell took instruction from and fellowshiped
with Adventists from 1868 through 1879, and quit the staff
of the Adventist publication *The Herald of the Morning* in
1879 to begin publishing his own magazine. So, Russell
was actually an Adventist at the time of his early writings.
Besides Jehovah's Witnesses, other sects that sprang from
the Adventist movement include the Seventh Day Adventists, the Advent Christian Church, the Church of God
(Faith of Abraham), and the Life and Advent Union.

Bible Students   The followers of Charles T. Russell
called themselves Bible Students. After his death this name
continued to be used, not only by those who stuck with the
Watchtower organization controlled by J. F. Rutherford but
also by splinter groups under the leadership of former Russell appointees. The name still applies to Russellite groups
such as the Dawn Bible Students and the Chicago Bible
Students. Rutherford had his followers adopt the name

Jehovah's Witnesses in 1931 to distinguish themselves from these others.

International Bible Students Association   In *The Watch Tower* of April 1, 1910, C. T. Russell instructed his followers in the United States and worldwide to identify themselves and advertise their meetings under this name. This is also the name of the British corporation formed by Russell in 1914, which continues to function under the direction of the parent corporation, the Watch Tower Bible and Tract Society of Pennsylvania.

Jehovah's Witnesses   Joseph Rutherford had congregations associated with the Watchtower organization adopt this name in 1931 to distinguish themselves from other Russellite groups that shared the designation Bible Students. But the organization has not incorporated under this name as a legal entity.

People's Pulpit Association   This legal corporation was formed in 1909 under the Membership Corporation Law of New York to care for operations in that state. It was renamed Watchtower Bible and Tract Society, Inc., in 1939, and then in 1956 it took on the present form of its name, Watchtower Bible and Tract Society of New York, Inc.

Second Adventist(s)   Referring to the return, or second advent, of Christ, this is another name for Adventists (see above).

Watchtower Bible and Tract Society of New York, Inc. Originally formed as the People's Pulpit Association, this New York legal corporation works under the direction of the parent Pennsylvania corporation, the Watch Tower Bible and Tract Society. The New York corporation is officially the branch organization in charge of activities in the United States.

Watch Tower Bible and Tract Society   Originally named Zion's Watch Tower Tract Society, this Pennsylvania corporation was formed in 1884 to carry on C. T. Russell's publishing work. It serves as the parent corporation for Jehovah's Witnesses worldwide. Various corporate bodies have been established in other lands, but all work under the direction of the Pennsylvania corporation. The primary purpose for the multiple corporations has been to meet the requirements for owning real estate under the various legal jurisdictions where the sect operates.

Endnotes

Chapter 1: Origins

1. Studies in the Scriptures, vol. 7, *The Finished Mystery*, 1917 edition, p. 53.
2. Studies in the Scriptures, vol. 7, *The Finished Mystery*, 1917 edition, p. 54.

Chapter 2: *An Overview*

1. Studies in the Scriptures, vol. 3, 1891, 1903 edition, p. 313.
2. *The Watch Tower*, May 15, 1925, p. 148.
3. *The Watch Tower*, November 15, 1928, p. 344.
4. *The Watch Tower*, November 15, 1928, pp. 344, 341.
5. A. H. Macmillan, *Faith on the March* (Englewood Cliffs: Prentice-Hall, 1957), p. 79.
6. *King's County Clerk's Index No. 15845—Year 1940*, N.Y. Supreme Court, Appellate Division, Second Department, Olin R. Moyle *versus* Fred W. Franz, Nathan H. Knorr, Grant Suiter, *et al.*, Case on Appeal, vol. 11, p. 795.
7. David A. Reed, ex-Witness and author of this present volume as well as other books on the sect, was formally tried and expelled in March 1982, as the organizational purge reached down into the local congregations of Jehovah's Witnesses.
8. *The Watchtower*, August 1, 1974, p. 464.
9. In Andersen's tale con men pose as tailors and announce that the new clothes they are making for the emperor will be appreciated by all except people unfit for their positions or hopelessly stupid. As a result, each of the emperor's deputies, although he sees no

clothes, speaks admiringly of what the "tailors" pretend to hold up and display; none wants to lose his position or be thought stupid. Finally, the emperor puts on the "clothes" (which he does not dare admit he cannot see after so many of his deputies have spoken admiringly of them) and shows them off in a public parade. Not wanting to be thought stupid, the crowds, too, shout approval of the emperor's new clothes, until a typically honest little child shouts out, "The emperor is naked!"

Chapter 3: *The Charles Taze Russell Era*

1. Studies in the Scriptures, vol. 7, *The Finished Mystery,* 1917 edition, p. 54.
2. *Apocalypse Delayed,* by M. James Penton (University of Toronto Press, 1985), p. 17.
3. *1975 Yearbook of Jehovah's Witnesses,* p. 36; *Watch Tower Publications Index 1930–1985,* p. 916; but the *Watch Tower Publications Index 1930–1960,* p. 306, assigns it the 1877 date.

Chapter 4: *The Joseph F. Rutherford Era*

1. Although admitting that Maria Russell lived apart from her husband for nearly twenty years, the Watchtower Society insists that this was merely "a legalized separation" and that no divorce took place. The *1975 Yearbook of Jehovah's Witnesses* cites a law dictionary to prove that the Russells' "In Divorce" decree handed down by a Pittsburgh court on March 4, 1908, was actually a "partial or qualified divorce" that "may more properly be termed a legal separation" (p. 67).
2. *Revelation, Its Grand Climax at Hand!* p. 120.
3. *Faith on the March,* by A. H. Macmillan, 1957, pp. 84–85; *The Watchtower,* September 1, 1989, p. 13; April 1, 1990, p. 31; *Awake!* April 22, 1990, p. 6.
4. *Apocalypse Delayed: The Story of Jehovah's Witnesses* (Toronto: University of Toronto Press, 1985), p. 225.

Chapter 5: *The Nathan H. Knorr Era*

1. The 1950 edition had *Originally* instead of *In [the] beginning.*
2. *The Watchtower,* January 1, 1954, p. 31.
3. By intentionally failing to capitalize *witnesses* Watchtower writers seek to convey the thought that followers are indeed the only people on earth who are truly witnesses of God, as opposed to simply being members of a sect named *Jehovah's Witnesses.*
4. "Moving Christ's *parousia* from 1874 to 1914—when?" by Kris Marlow, *Comments from the Friends,* Winter 1992, pp. 14–15.

Bibliography

Watchtower Publications

(These are not listed here, since they are listed chronologically in the main body of this book.)

Critical Works

Arellano, Angel. *Exposing "Should You Believe in the Trinity?"* (self-published, 1990).

Barefoot, Darek. *Jehovah's Witnesses and the Hour of Darkness.* Grand Junction, Colorado: Grand Valley Press, 1992.

Bowman, Robert M., Jr. *Why You Should Believe in the Trinity.* Grand Rapids: Baker Book House, 1990.

Countess, Robert H. *The Jehovah's Witnesses' New Testament.* Phillipsburg: Presbyterian and Reformed Publishing Company, 1982, 1987.

Franz, Raymond V. *Crisis of Conscience,* Atlanta: Commentary Press, 1983.

Jonsson, Carl Olof. *The Gentile Times Reconsidered.* Atlanta: Commentary Press, 1986.

Penton, M. James. *Apocalypse Delayed: The Story of Jehovah's Witnesses.* Toronto: University of Toronto Press, 1985.

Reed, David A. *Jehovah's Witnesses Answered Verse by Verse.* Grand Rapids: Baker Book House, 1986.

Reed, David A., ed. *Index of Watchtower Errors.* Compiled by Steve Huntoon and John Cornell. Grand Rapids: Baker Book House, 1990.

Readers interested in obtaining originals or reproductions of out-of-print Watchtower materials and other books listed here that are not available through bookstores may direct their inquiries to the author:

David A. Reed
Comments from the Friends
P.O. Box 840
Stoughton, MA 02072

Subject Index

201

Scripture Index

(See also Chapter 8, "Watchtower Bible Commentaries.")